A BIRD'S-EYE VIEW

My Mostly Wonderful, Always Unforgettable Half-Century with the Eagles

Leo Carlin with Paul Domowitch

TRIUMPH
BOOKS

Library of Congress Cataloging-in-Publication Data available upon request.

This book is available in quantity at special discounts for your group or organization. For further information, contact:

Triumph Books LLC
814 North Franklin Street
Chicago, Illinois 60610
(312) 337-0747
www.triumphbooks.com

Printed in U.S.A.
ISBN: 978-1-62937-846-6
Design by Patricia Frey

Photos pp. 39 and 83 courtesy of AP Images; pp. 202 and 208 courtesy of the coauthor; pp. 19, 25, 39, 45, 114, 121, 176, 211, 216, and 217 courtesy of the Philadelphia Eagles. All other photos are courtesy of the Carlin family.

To my dear wife, Kay, who sacrificed so much during my career. Your love, support, encouragement, and perseverance are an example to all. You are the love of my life and my hero and I thank you from the bottom of my heart.—L.C.

To Shelley, my unbelievable wife, who has been there at my side for the last 40 years, adroitly coping with a sportswriter's crazy life. And to my two wonderful daughters, Allison and Amy, who brighten our lives and still regularly ask me whether I regret not having a son. The answer is an unequivocal no.—P.D.

Contents

Foreword

When I purchased the Philadelphia Eagles in 1994, Leo Carlin was already entrenched as our ticket manager. It was an area of the business that I knew very little about at the time, but I had heard great things about Leo, and I knew that having somebody with his experience would be vital to our success as an organization.

Leo and I had a wonderful relationship from the beginning. He was very passionate about building and maintaining a strong relationship with our season-ticket holders, treating them like family and keeping open lines of communication with them. If you had a question or needed to get in touch with somebody about tickets, it was always, "Where's Leo?" He was, and remains, a wonderful ambassador for our organization.

Before we moved from Veterans Stadium to Lincoln Financial Field in 2003, one of our major priorities as we designed the new stadium was how the layout of the new facility was going to affect each individual season-ticket holder. People may not know how much time and energy go into a project like that, but because the seating arrangements were going to be very different, we had to make sure we had a process that would be as fair as possible for everyone.

Leo was the public face of this very time-consuming project. The work was endless, and the reason he was able to do such an outstanding job with it is the same reason he was such an important member of our front office: he truly cared about the fans and our relationship with them. Not only did Leo successfully move Eagles season-ticket holders into Lincoln Financial Field, he had already done the same thing 30 years earlier when the team moved from Franklin Field to Veterans Stadium!

To be a part of the Eagles organization for more than a half-century—to be an integral part of *any* business for that long—you have to care deeply about your work. Leo just wanted to make us better and better. You don't know who you're inheriting when you buy a business, but Leo was a rock and someone who was an excellent resource to me because of his breadth and depth of knowledge about our football team. Everybody in the building knew him. When you passed Leo in the hallways and asked how he was doing, he always gave a signature reply: "Sterling!" We all appreciated his cheerful demeanor and enthusiasm.

Football is a unique business, especially here in Philadelphia, where our fans are so avid. We have almost 70,000 passionate supporters every time we play a game at our stadium. With almost 20,000 season-ticket holder accounts and 70,000 clients, it can be very difficult to establish and maintain a relationship on any personal level. But Leo humanized that relationship-building throughout his entire tenure with the team—from Franklin Field to Veterans Stadium to Lincoln Financial Field. He was so passionate about being able to please and service all of our customers in a one-on-one manner. He helped create a bond among our community that is very unique in any business that serves so many people.

We inducted Leo into the Philadelphia Eagles Hall of Fame in 2012. That's an honor we reserve only for the most deserving individuals who have greatly affected the organization for the better. For us it was an easy decision to make because of how tremendous Leo's contributions had been and how valuable they would continue to be. Everyone in the Eagles organization appreciates Leo's loyalty, his personality, his warmth, and his upbeat approach to work every day in a business that has so many ups and downs.

One thing that always struck me about Leo is how humble and thankful he is for his time with the Eagles. But what he doesn't realize is just how lucky we are to have had him as a member of this organization for so many years. In today's world, that's remarkable. He had a very special career, and I will always be thankful that he has been a part of the Eagles family for so many decades.

—Jeffrey Lurie, owner, Philadelphia Eagles

Foreword

Since 1987 I've been associated with the National Football League—first as a player, then as a broadcaster. It's been an incredible honor and privilege, and yet my career probably never would have materialized if it weren't for the intercession of my dear friend Leo Carlin. I first met Leo when I was a teenager. I was fortunate enough to attend high school in Philadelphia at his alma mater, St. Joseph's Prep, where I played football with three of Leo's sons.

After high school, I attended the University of Delaware. When I was a senior there, I was drafted by the New England Patriots. I was a quarterback at Delaware, but the Patriots wanted to convert me to either a running back or defensive back. I realized that my chances of making an NFL team at a position I had never played weren't very good. Even before calling my agent, I called the one person I knew who would give me good, sound advice and maybe even help get me out of this mess: Leo Carlin.

Little did I know when I called him for advice after the draft that Leo was good friends with Bucko Kilroy, who was the Patriots' vice president and pro personnel director at the time. Kilroy was a former player and scout with the Eagles, and part of his career there had intersected with Leo's.

Leo reached out to Bucko immediately, and less than a week later I was traded to the Minnesota Vikings, where I eventually earned a roster spot... as a quarterback. Believe me when I say this never would have happened if it weren't for Leo making that call, and for that I am forever grateful to this generous man. Leo has done countless favors for friends and colleagues during the course of a career in professional football that has spanned more than half a century.

Leo is a Philadelphia icon—not only for what he means to the Eagles but for how he treats people: with genuine love and respect. Leo joined the Eagles in 1960 and moved the team and its fans to three different stadiums for several different owners, head coaches, and general managers. You can probably count on one hand the number of people (other than team owners) who have spent more than 50 years with one NFL franchise. You don't last that long in this business if you aren't great at what you do and well respected by your peers.

Leo Carlin was the best in the business and wasn't just respected and admired but was loved and adored by everyone associated with the Eagles and the NFL. That's why he was nominated for induction into the Pro Football Hall of Fame multiple times, and why he was inducted into the Eagles Hall of Fame in 2012.

More important than the honors and accolades, though, is the essence of a man whose character and integrity comprise the foundation of a life spent helping others. Faith, family, and football are what Leo Carlin has always been about. I have learned so much from this humble man simply by watching and observing how he has spent his life in service to others. Leo has been a humble servant his entire life, and there is no better role model in our great game! While Leo has certainly left a lasting legacy with the Philadelphia Eagles and the National Football League, what is even more significant to me is the example he has set—for myself and others—of what it truly means to be a man. I have been blessed to call him my friend and mentor.

I know you will enjoy this book for its stories, anecdotes, and behind-the-scenes look at a pioneer who was involved in so much of the history of the Philadelphia Eagles, from their 1960 championship season right up to their recent Super Bowl championship in 2018.

—*Rich Gannon, CBS Sports broadcaster,*
four-time Pro Bowl quarterback

Coauthor's Note

To say this book has been a long time in the making would be an understatement. It was 11 years ago that Leo first mentioned to me that he wanted to write his memoirs and wondered if I'd be interested in helping him. The easy part was saying yes. Leo was a longtime friend, and given his long history with the Eagles and pro football, I knew he would have a lot of great stories to tell about his life and his long career in Philadelphia. The hard part was actually getting the project done. For 11 years, in between football seasons and drafts and OTAs and training camps and hip replacements and graduations and births and deaths and marriages, we chipped away at it. I've watched Leo battle a hideous disease—Parkinson's—that he didn't have when we began all this. His determination to fight it, even though he knows it will eventually get in the last punch, has been one of the most inspiring things I've ever seen, right up there with his wife, Kay's, own valiant health battle against an infection that has ravaged her body for the better part of the last quarter-century.

This book will take you through more than five decades of Eagles history with Leo as the unforgettable tour guide. It will take you through his three years with the USFL's Philadelphia Stars. It will take you through ownership changes, the firing of coaches, championship seasons, and losing seasons. It's been an honor working on this project with Leo. I hope you enjoy reading this book as much I enjoyed writing it.

—Paul Domowitch

Chapter 1

In the Beginning

I'm just a kid from North Philly. The streets of Hunting Park were my playground growing up, the alleys my hiding places. Our house was near Broad and Pike, which back then was a predominantly Irish Catholic neighborhood.

Like most kids, I loved sports. I played them all. But for as long as I can remember, football was my true love, my passion. It was the one dominant factor in my childhood. Actually, as you're about to learn, it's been the dominant factor in my entire life.

I was a small kid, and truth be told, I wasn't a particularly good football player. But I never let that deter me. I loved the game. I played it on the North Philly sandlots and in high school at St. Joe's Prep. I even played later in life in Philadelphia-area rough-touch leagues, which probably wasn't the smartest thing for a 5'9", 150-pound guy supporting a wife and seven kids to do. After I graduated from college—of course, another Catholic school, St. Joe's College (now St. Joe's University)—I was lucky enough to get a job with my hometown pro football team, the Philadelphia Eagles. I guess you could say the rest is history.

I worked for the Eagles for 50-plus years before finally retiring in April 2015. Three years before I rode off into the sunset at the age of 77, I got the gift of a lifetime when I was inducted into the Eagles Hall of Fame. Well, that was actually the first of *two* gifts of a lifetime. The second came

My parents, Anna and Lex.

My childhood home in North Philly, 1344 North Pike Place.

two years after I retired, when the Eagles won their first Super Bowl title. Even though I was no longer with the team on a daily basis at that point, owner Jeffrey Lurie was thoughtful enough to give me a Super Bowl ring.

Imagine that. This kid from North Philly is in the same honored place with the likes of Eagles football legends such as Steve Van Buren, Chuck Bednarik, Reggie White, Harold Carmichael, Bill Bergey, Tom Brookshier, Tommy McDonald, and Brian Dawkins. Is that crazy or what?

I've truly had a wonderful life. I've been married to the love of my life, Kay, for 60 years. We raised seven terrific children and have 22 grandchildren. And I spent my entire adult life working in professional football. Yeah, I guess you could say I've been a pretty lucky guy.

Growing up, we were your basic Irish Catholic family of that era. Our parish was St. Stephen's, which was right around the corner from our house. I was an altar boy at St. Stephen's, and living so close to the church meant that I was always on call. Anytime an altar boy didn't show up for the 6:00 AM Mass, guess who got the phone call to fill in? That's right: me.

When the phone would ring early in the morning, I'd say, "Ma, tell 'em to get somebody else. I'm tired." But it never worked. My mother, a devout Catholic, never was going to tell the priest that her son was too tired to serve Mass, especially since the pastor at St. Stephen's also happened to be the bishop of the diocese. I became one of the "special" altar boys. I'd get called for all of the special Masses.

As I mentioned earlier, I attended high school at St. Joe's Prep (referred to most often as "the Prep"). So did both of my older brothers and all four of my sons. Three of my grandsons also went to the Prep. People ask me, "Did you like the Prep?" I say, "Well, let me put it this way: I went there. All of my boys went there. My brothers went there. My cousin went there. My grandkids went there. So yeah, I guess I like the Prep."

I knew I was going to the Prep from the time I was three years old. My brothers, who were 12 and 13 years older than me, went there. I don't know if that's what influenced me or not, but there never was any debate—that's where I was going. My father was very proud that we went there. Tuition was about $200 a year, which back then was a lot of money. But he always found a way to come up with it.

Me (24) during my playing days at St. Joe's Prep.

Graduation day at St. Joe's Prep.
All four of my sons
followed me to St. Joe's.

I remember when I first got there, I ran into this guy named Franny Delano. I asked him where he was from, and he said Narberth. At the time, I had never heard of it. I was thinking, *Narberth? I must be the poorest kid in this school.* But I got involved in sports and eventually realized I wasn't the only kid at Prep who didn't have a lot of money. Somehow, though, it worked out pretty well.

I started working for the Eagles in April 1960. I had been discharged from the United States Marine Corps and needed a job. Kay and I had gotten married a few months earlier. The team was looking for a part-timer to help distribute tickets; it turned out to be the opportunity of a lifetime.

I guess the ticket business was kind of in my blood already. My dad ran the Apollo Theater in Atlantic City for a while. My oldest brother, Lex, ran the Forrest Theater in Philadelphia for a long time. And my other brother, Joe, was the manager of the Walnut Street Theater, also in Philly.

I was kind of considered the black sheep of my family for going to work for a sports team as opposed to a theater, but I never regretted it.

The altar boy
of St. Stephen's.

For a while, the Carlins had a monopoly on the entertainment industry in Philadelphia. The Eagles, the theaters—if you needed a ticket, we were the people to call.

I still remember the first time I walked into the Eagles' offices, which were located at 15th and Locust back then. There were tickets all over the place, so I knew they needed help. Keep in mind this was long before computers.

It was a different time back then. The Eagles' ticket manager was Ed Doyle. Every day, after a whiskey sour lunch, he would nod off at his desk until it was time to leave. Meanwhile, the rest of us would work our asses off trying to service our customers. Doyle didn't care about the customers. In fact, when he wasn't sleeping, he'd sit there and insult them. I wound up being a full-time part-timer in the ticket office for three years.

Back when I first went to work in the Eagles' ticket office, pro football wasn't the huge deal it is today. They played their home games at Franklin Field on the campus of the University of Pennsylvania. Back then, Penn's football team typically drew more fans than the Eagles.

But the 1960 championship game against the Green Bay Packers changed all that. That game drew 67,000 fans. Franklin Field only had 60,658 seats, but we added temporary stands for the game and filled every one of them. The Eagles won their third NFL championship in 13 years, beating the Packers 17–13. Who knew it would be 57 years before they would win another one?

The Eagles didn't have one owner when I went to work for them in 1960; they had 100 of them. They were owned by an investment group called the Happy Hundred, headed by Philadelphia trucking magnate James P. Clark. Clark and his group had bought the team from Lex Thompson in January 1949, right after the Eagles won their second straight NFL championship. The purchase price was $250,000. Today the Eagles are worth more than *$3 billion*! Unbelievable.

The organization was a bit ethnically lopsided in those days. Let me run down some of the names of the people who ran the Eagles organization back then: McNamee, McNally, Donahue, Doyle, Hogan, O'Connell, McGloughlin, and Gallagher. I remember when they hired a girl by the name of Jerkowitz once—everybody was in a state of shock. Diversity didn't exist.

There was a lot of power in the organization back then—not necessarily on the field but in local politics. Many people in the organization were well-connected to the Democratic Party. I remember one day not long after I started with the Eagles, one of our investors got caught running booze across the state line. He came in to get help from the team's executive vice president, a guy named Joe Donahue. Joe's nickname was Jiggs because he looked like the titular character from the comic strip *Jiggs and Maggie*. He even was married to a woman named Margaret.

Jiggs was a charming man with a booming voice. When the investor came in for help, Jiggs got on the phone to David Lawrence, who just happened to be the governor of Pennsylvania at the time. You could hear him all over the office. He said, "David, me boy. Someone here wants to make a contribution to the party." That was the last anybody ever heard about the investor's brush with the law.

The Eagles' organizational setup was a bit weird compared to a normal corporate structure. For example, the president of the Eagles also was the fire commissioner for the city of Philadelphia. He would stop by every now and then with this horribly stern look on his face and have a short session with Jiggs, and then not come back for days on end. Not exactly a full-time job. I never understood it. Obviously, there was some political reasoning behind it.

In the ticket business, preparing for a season is more difficult than going through one. So I would go back to that dingy office at 15th and Locust every May and begin the long process—remember, no computers yet—of preparing and distributing the tickets for the upcoming season. It was a huge task and one that took all summer working both day and night.

I saw the game of football from a unique perspective during my tenure. I'm not talking about the action on the field; I'm talking about inside the front office, where I worked for more than half a century. I worked for four different owners during my many years with the Eagles: Jerry Wolman, Leonard Tose, Norman Braman, and Jeffrey Lurie. I ran the team's ticket operation and also served as the Eagles' business manager in the 1960s and '70s. I left the Eagles for three years in the early 1980s and was the business manager for the Philadelphia Stars of the United States Football League, where I worked for a fifth owner, Myles Tanenbaum. In this book, I'll give you some insight into what it was like working for those five men and the interesting experiences I've had, and the people I've met along the way.

Chapter 2
Jerry and Ed

Prior to the 1960s, professional football ranked a distant third in popularity to baseball and college football. As I mentioned earlier, Penn used to regularly outdraw the Eagles at Franklin Field. But that started to change after the Eagles' win over the Packers in 1960—not just in Philadelphia but all over the country. Professional football started to become more and more popular.

In 1964 Jerry Wolman came roaring into town from Washington, D.C.—bringing with him a lawyer by the name of Earl Foreman and the dynamic Ed Snider—and bought the Eagles from the Happy Hundred. Jerry, who was from Shenandoah in upstate Pennsylvania, was just 36 years old and extremely likeable. He was the youngest owner in the NFL when he bought the Eagles.

Wolman's was a rags-to-riches success story. He was a high school dropout who worked in his father's fruit business and eventually built a successful career in construction and real estate. He owned several office buildings and apartments in Washington, D.C., and was worth nearly $40 million when he bought the Eagles for $5.5 million. For all his money, Jerry always acted like the kid from Shenandoah. He hated it when someone would address him as Mr. Wolman. "Call me Jerry," he would always say.

I remember the first time Jerry saw our offices at 15th and Locust. He walked through the front door, walked into the men's room, walked out, and said, "We're moving." True to Jerry's promise, we moved. We took over the first floor of the building at 30th and Market, which housed the *Evening Bulletin* newspaper at the time. He got new furniture, new decor, new everything—including a huge wallpaper picture of the view of the game from the east stands at nearby Franklin Field. Franklin Field was/is a great place to watch a game, though it obviously pales in comparison to today's state-of-the-art stadiums.

Ed Snider—who later would become the owner of the city's hockey team, the Flyers—was part of Wolman's investment group when he bought the Eagles. Ed was given a 7 percent share of the team and was named the team's vice president and treasurer. Yet few people realize Eddie pretty much ran the Eagles in those early days.

In the summer of 1964, when I was still a part-timer, and after Wolman had moved the team's offices to 30th and Market, I was asked to come back and work. I refused. I loved the game, loved working for an NFL team, but I couldn't stand the ticket-office situation anymore. The ineptitude and laziness I had to deal with every day there had become intolerable. The disorganization, the backstabbing—I just couldn't take it anymore. So I declined to come back.

I couldn't understand why this dynamic new ownership would tolerate a situation like that in what I considered a very important part of the organization. I mean, we were dealing with millions of dollars. As it turned out, I didn't give Jerry and Ed enough credit. They knew what was going on. Ed swept in and went into action. The ticket manager suddenly became "ill" and left abruptly. Ed discovered many improprieties. I still remember him sitting on the floor of the ticket office in his stocking feet at 7:00 PM one night sorting out tickets that were supposed to be sold but were actually being hoarded for personal reasons. The ticket manager eventually was fired, as was his assistant, and Snider offered me the job of full-time ticket manager.

I was thrilled. The organization under Jerry Wolman was, for the most part, a big party—probably too much of one at times. But it was the beginning of a lot of fun. I threw myself into the job and worked my ass off. It was lot of work getting things organized, but thanks to Jerry and Ed, it also was gratifying.

In 1966 we had a rare winning season. We went 9–5 and finished tied for second in the Eastern Conference with Cleveland. Dallas won the East and played the Western Conference winner, the Green Bay Packers, for the NFL championship. The Packers won 34–27.

We then got to play in what they called the Playoff Bowl, a meaningless consolation game between the two conference runners-up. We played the Baltimore Colts down in Miami's Orange Bowl. Jerry took everybody in the organization and their spouses down to Florida for the game and treated us to everything. I can still remember signing "Cabana 5" to almost everything. It was a one-week party that ended with the Colts beating us 20–14 in a game that didn't matter.

At the time, Kay and I had four children. About nine months after that trip to Miami, our fifth was born. Since we had stayed at the Ivanhoe Hotel, people suggested we should have named our fifth child Ivan instead of Christopher. Yes, that was quite a week.

While we were down there, I got a call from Sonny Werblin, who owned the New York Jets. He lived in South Florida and asked me to come over to his house for breakfast to discuss some changes I'd made to the Eagles' ticketing process.

I was the first one in the NFL to computerize ticketing. It wasn't very sophisticated, but it was better than the way we had been doing things. I used a guy from a Washington, D.C., accounting firm. Then a guy who owned a computer company in Baltimore started working with us to enhance and change the system in ticket offices and make them more computer-friendly. It didn't mean all the tickets disappeared and we didn't have to do anything manually anymore, but it made things easier.

Other teams eventually saw how I was doing it and started to go in that direction. Anyway, Werblin had heard about it and wanted to talk to me.

Boy, was the kid from North Philly nervous. Mrs. Werblin served me my orange juice. How awkward was that for a young ticket manager from Philadelphia? During our discussion, Sonny held up a copy of the *New York Times*. There was a picture of a young Jets player on the sports page. Sonny said, "He hasn't even played a down for us yet and he still manages to get me great publicity." The kid's name was Joe Willie Namath.

Working for Jerry Wolman was never dull; he had a beautiful, fun-loving personality. One day I was in my office on the phone, and suddenly I jumped up on my desk. Why? Because our goofy owner had brought a real, live lion into my office. It wasn't fully grown, but I'm not sure the lion knew that. Jerry laughed and laughed when he saw me standing on top of my desk. Someone had given him the lion as a present. Seriously. He eventually took it home to his wife, Ann. But as it got bigger, they had to donate it to a zoo.

Jerry was generous to a fault. I once saw him go up to a paperboy and buy all of his papers. But Jerry only took one paper so the kid could sell the rest and keep the money.

I remember being invited to Jerry's son Allen's bar mitzvah down in Washington, D.C. What a party! I'm Catholic and from North Philly and had never seen anything like it. At first I didn't think I would be able to go, because I had to work that day. So Kay went down with friends of ours. I was in the office alone, working, when the phone rang. It was Jerry. In the midst of all the entertaining he had to do, he called me to tell me he was sending a private plane to meet me and take me down to Allen's bar mitzvah. There I was, flying copilot. The head of our player personnel department at the time also was on the plane. The thing I remember was our pilot was a substitute because Jerry had invited his regular pilot to the celebration.

Jerry had a limo at the airport to greet us when we landed, and he paid for everything. What a weekend! It was typical Jerry Wolman. He could've had other people make the arrangements, but he wanted to do it personally. He made two phone calls to us on the way down just to make sure everything was OK.

The big three in the organization back then were Jerry, Ed Snider—who was a tremendous businessman and would become a good friend of mine—and Earl Foreman, the lawyer Jerry had brought with him from D.C., who was also Snider's brother-in-law. Ed and Earl both were part of Jerry's original investment group. They took Philadelphia by storm. The party atmosphere and the working environment were terrific.

It all came crashing down in 1969, though Wolman's financial empire had started to spring leaks a couple years earlier. He was building the John Hancock Center in Chicago, a 100-story steel-and-glass edifice that Jerry described as a "city in the sky." It was going to be the world's second-tallest skyscraper and would be Jerry's legacy. But an engineering miscalculation with the foundation caused major delays that drained Wolman's fortune, sent him into bankruptcy, and forced him to sell his beloved Eagles.

Chapter 3
Jerry's Decline and Fall

Jerry Wolman had big plans when he came to Philadelphia in 1964. He bought the Eagles. He wanted to bring a hockey franchise to the city. He was building a new arena that would house the hockey team. He bought the Yellow Cab taxi company. And he wanted to build a city within a city on the other side of the Delaware River in Camden.

There was a hotel, restaurant, and bar at 39th and Chestnut at the time called Chestnut Hall. It was owned by Jerry and Ed Snider and their group. This was right at the beginning of the sexual revolution. I think a lot went on there that I wasn't privy to. A man named Ronnie Pollock was put in charge of it. Everything in the place was called Ronnie's. There was Ronnie's Bar. The lunchroom was called Ronnie's Side Pocket. The billiard room was called Ronnie's Pool Hall. I don't think the ladies' room was called Ronnie's, but I couldn't swear to it.

There was a basketball court at the hotel. A lot of people from the Eagles and a bunch of Eddie's friends would get together and play after hours. I was never much of a basketball player, but I had one thing I could do really well: I could run up against a wall, propel myself into the air, and dunk the ball. Years later, whenever Ed would introduce me to anyone, he would say, "This is Leo Carlin. He can dunk a basketball." They'd look at this 5'9" guy standing in front of them and be more than a little skeptical.

One day Ed and I were at Ronnie's Side Pocket having lunch, and Ed was being a little tough on Ronnie. He thought the roast beef was being cut a little too thick, or something like that. Next thing I knew, Ed fired him and Ronnie was out on the street.

A few months later, we were all in a room at Chestnut Hall trying to come up with a name for the new arena, which would eventually be called the Spectrum. Hal Freeman, who had been named the president of the new arena, wanted to call it the Keystone, which wouldn't have been a bad name since Pennsylvania is the Keystone State. But his presentation was far outdone by that of Lou Scheinfeld, who suggested the Spectrum name. Lou would become the founding vice president of the Flyers and the president of the Spectrum, and in 1980 he would be named the chief executive officer of the 76ers basketball team. Anyway, Lou had brought along a board with the eight letters in the name on it, each of them standing for something—S for *sports*, P for *people*, E for *entertainment*, C for *concerts*, and so on.

While everyone was voting, a guy named Jack Edelstein walked in. Jack was a semi-comedian and a legendary playboy. He had once dated Marilyn Monroe. He had a great sense of humor. Ed asked him for his opinion on the name for the new arena. Jack thought about it for a few seconds and then said, "Why don't you call it Ronnie's?" I thought Ed was going to lunge out of his seat and kill him.

The Spectrum opened in March 1967. Not long after, Wolman's financial empire started to collapse. He tried to borrow money from everybody. By 1968 the situation had become pretty bleak. Jerry had spread himself too thin and cash was scarce. At one point, he tried to go public with a package that included the Eagles, the Flyers, the Spectrum, and some other assets that he had, but that attempt didn't work.

He did a lot of things to try and get money to stay afloat. He even borrowed money using Eagles tickets as collateral. Believe it or not, some lawyer—I can't remember the guy's name—even went for it for a while. I hated the idea. Just think of what would have happened if the season came and all of the fans' tickets and ticket money were tied up with some lender. The town would have gone nuts. They would have torn down the Eagles offices brick by brick. Jerry, God rest his soul, was a great guy. But he was sinking badly and he was desperate. And desperate people do desperate things.

By that point, Jerry and Ed Snider had grown apart. In Jerry's 2010 autobiography, written three years before his death, he said he had needed collateral to obtain financing to keep everything together. But his two partners—Snider and Earl Foreman, who was married to Ed's sister—refused to sign over their shares.

When the Eagles played at Franklin Field, I used to go the office at 30th and Market before the game to get all of my ticket records. It was a pain in the ass, but that's the way it was then. One Sunday, I got to the office and the lights were on. When I went to see who was there, I found Jerry, surrounded by paperwork. We talked for a while and then the phone rang. It was an overseas operator. It was a call from one of Jerry's buddies, who was over in Europe somewhere trying to get financing so Jerry could keep his empire together. When Jerry finally hung up, he got very emotional and said to me, "We got the money."

I assumed he meant he had gotten someone from overseas to invest in the Eagles and Flyers. But then he said, "I need someone to go to Los Angeles tonight." There I was, the only other person in the office, and the boss was asking for a volunteer to get on a plane and fly across the country. I reluctantly agreed to go. Then he told me what he needed me to do. I was going to be picking up $50 million. Sending me out to L.A. to get $50 million was crazy and impetuous and clearly an act of desperation. But like I said, desperate people do desperate things.

I went to work at Franklin Field that day. We played the game. I can't remember who we played or whether we won. I had other things on my mind. After the game, I showered at the stadium. I had called Kay, and she brought me a suit. Jerry and I then got in a car and drove to New York. When we got there, I was taken, along with Jerry, to an apartment where there was a man they called "the Doctor." I'm not making this up. There were papers all over the place. Eventually they packed them up, gave them to me, and drove me to the airport for the flight to L.A. to pick up $50 million. That's a lot of money in any year, but this was 1968. All I had was the paperwork in my briefcase and an address. I flew out of LaGuardia to Atlanta to Dallas and finally to L.A. Yes, it was a very long night.

When I got to L.A., I found a cab and gave the driver the address. He gave me a curious look when he saw where I wanted to go. He drove to a depressed area of the city. I was expecting to go to a luxurious office in a luxurious building to pick up the $50 million. This was literally a corner-store type of place with a sign outside.

There was one lawyer inside. After three hours of waiting and a lot of useless dialogue, he told me he couldn't review the papers I had brought and that the bank wasn't going to be able to do the wire transfer and that I might as well go home. That was OK by me. I couldn't get out of there fast enough. I found a kid on the street who said he could drive, and I had him take me back to LAX and took a flight back to Philly.

The next day I was over at the restaurant in the Spectrum, which was called the Blue Line. Ed Snider came in and asked me where I'd been. I told him about my weird trip to L.A. He said there never was any money, that it might've been an extortion plot since there were several payments by Jerry that were listed as so-called "expenses" to people supposedly trying to arrange financing for him.

Ed told me I was going to hear things. I said I already had heard things. He said, "Well, you're going to hear more." The next day Jerry fired Eddie. As a result of his termination, Eddie wound up with 60 percent of the Flyers, which turned into 100 percent after he got done buying some other people out. Eddie did one of the city's greatest marketing jobs with the Flyers, taking a sport very few people in Philadelphia cared a crap about to a level of popularity no one ever could have imagined.

Eddie and I were good friends. He offered me jobs maybe 200 times over the years for his various entities, including the Flyers and Spectacor,

With Eagles GM Pete Retzlaff (left) and Sig Ettinger (right) in 1970.

now Comcast Spectacor. He was dynamic. He didn't like getting up in the morning, but when he arrived at work, it was intense. He had an aura about him—and I used to talk to him about this—that made everybody concentrate on what they were doing. He would walk past your desk and it would be business right away, even if you were in the middle of a humorous conversation. That's the way he was, even though he was only thirty-some years old at the time.

Jerry's desperate fight to hang on to his beloved Eagles ended on May 1, 1969, the day he officially sold the team to Leonard Tose. Jerry left the office that day in tears. He called me at home that evening and apologized for not saying good-bye. He was crying uncontrollably and vowed to me that he would get the team back someday. He told me he had a deal with Tose that allowed him to buy back the Eagles if he came up with the money in a certain period of time. But it never happened.

Jerry went back to Washington, D.C., after the sale. He eventually made a financial comeback, and in 1998 he made an unsuccessful bid to buy the Redskins, losing out to current owner Dan Snyder. That was too bad for both Jerry and Redskins fans. Washington has made the playoffs only four times in the 20-plus years Snyder has owned the team. Leonard never would have given the team back to Jerry, anyway. When Tose finally sold it to Norman Braman in 1985 for $65 million—nearly $50 million more than he had paid—it was for the same reason Jerry had sold the team: he was broke.

The value of NFL teams just keeps going up. Braman sold the Eagles to Jeffrey Lurie for $185 million nine years after he bought it from Tose for a third of that. Today, nearly a quarter-century after Jeffrey bought the team, the Eagles are worth more than $3 billion, with a *B!* The Dallas Cowboys are worth $5.5 billion. The New England Patriots are worth $4.1 billion! It's crazy.

The league's television revenue continues to skyrocket. Each of the league's 32 teams receives $255 million a year from TV deals with Disney

(ABC and ESPN), CBS, Fox, NBC, and DirecTV. That's a 150 percent increase from 2010, when they received just below $100 million a year.

In 2018 Fox agreed to pay $3 billion a year for the next five years for the rights to *Thursday Night Football*, on top of the $1.1 billion they were paying for the rights to Sunday NFC games. "Opportunities likes these come along very infrequently," Peter Rice, the president of 21st Century Fox, said when asked why the company was willing to pay so much for the Thursday night package, which the league actually had considered doing away with at one point. "You either have the rights to the most watched content in media, and if you lose that action and don't take the opportunity, it won't come along for another five years."

The popularity of the game is beyond belief. The Eagles have a season-ticket waiting list of more than 50,000. When I first started with them in 1960, we sold 19,000 season tickets, which was considered really good. Then it increased to 30,000 and has kept growing. The Eagles' Super Bowl parade drew something like 3 million people. There is an insatiable appetite for pro football. There are games on Sunday, Monday, Thursday and, late in the season, even Saturday. Super Bowl LIV was watched by a mind-blowing 113.4 million people. The league's annual revenue is pushing $20 billion. From a fan perspective, the Eagles have premium services, club seating, the Touchdown Club at $800 per seat per game, the Eagles Television Network, and nonstop promotions. Pro football is a cash cow.

In a way, though, it's a little sad. The game has become such a big business that we forget sometimes that it's still a game. We would sit in a conference room every week and go around the room and discuss the business aspects of the Eagles, and the one word you would never hear is *football*. Still, nearly five years after my retirement, I remain addicted to the game and to the team I spent more than half a century working for.

Chapter 4

Joe K. and the 15-Year Contract

As a part-timer during the Happy Hundred regime, before Jerry Wolman bought the team, I mainly handled tickets, making sure the right people got the right tickets, doing it all by hand—pulling them out of a rack or box, addressing the envelopes, and sending them out to season-ticket holders before the first game.

I also worked the ticket window and waited on customers when they came to make their payments for season tickets. It was tedious work, and very difficult. I had to go to the bank every day because people didn't use credit cards back then. They would either pay by check or cash. We would process every payment on a little index card we had for each season-ticket holder. Those little index cards essentially were our season-ticket database in 1960.

Frankly, I hated it. But by 1964, when I was hired full-time, everything was much better. I really loved working for the Eagles. Things were much different in those days, more casual. You could walk into the coaches' rooms and strike up a conversation with them. I remember one time I stopped by Joe Kuharich's office. It was Joe's first season as the team's head coach. He was watching film of a previous game. It was our team in punt formation. Our punter at the time also happened to be our quarterback, King Hill.

I really liked King. I turned to Joe and did something you wouldn't even think of doing today. I said, "You know, I've often wondered why, in a punt situation like that, with the quarterback being your punter, why you don't just fake the punt and have him throw it." Well, sure enough, the next game, there we were, lined up in punt formation with King. But King didn't punt. He threw the ball to one of our receivers—I can't remember who it was—for a first down. We went on to win the game.

The next day in his press conference, when he was asked about the fake punt by reporters, Joe said, "Well, I saw by the way they lined up that we could pull it off." Joe never mentioned that I had suggested the idea to him, though I can't blame him. It would reflect poorly on a football coach to say, "Oh, I got that play from my ticket manager." I don't think I ever told King my role in that play. I retired with a 1.000 batting average in play-calling.

Prior to hiring Kuharich for the 1964 season, the Eagles had won a total of five games during the previous two seasons under Nick Skorich. After Kuharich's first Eagles team went 6–8 in 1964, Wolman was so pleased with the improvement that he rewarded Joe with a 15-year contract in 1965, just a year after hiring him. That's right, a 15-year contract—five years longer than the one the Raiders gave Jon Gruden a couple years back and two years longer than Bryce Harper's deal with the Phillies. The long deal was all Jerry. He did it quickly and quietly, and very few people in the organization—including Snider—even knew about it until after the fact.

The contract had everybody around the league scratching their heads. I remember one owner—I can't remember who—was quoted at the time as saying he wouldn't give God a 15-year NFL contract. I mean, Kuharich wasn't even considered one of the game's great coaches when the Eagles hired him. Early in his career, he led the University of San Francisco to an undefeated record. But aside from that, he didn't have a lot of success.

He went from USF to the Chicago Cardinals, where he succeeded Curly Lambeau as the head coach. He was there just one year, finishing 4–8. George Preston Marshall, who was the Washington Redskins' owner back then, hired him in 1954. He spent five years with the Redskins and had just one winning season. He left the Redskins to become the head coach at Notre Dame. The Irish had had just one losing season in the previous 25 years before Joe got there. In Joe's four years there, they finished 5–5 three times and 2–8 once. He resigned in the spring of 1963 and was replaced by Hugh Devore for a season before the school hired a fellow named Ara Parseghian. The rest is history.

I got along with Kuharich, but he was one of the least popular coaches in the history of the franchise. Joe instituted a no-fraternization rule when he became the Eagles' coach. He prohibited his players from dating any of the organization's female employees. At least one player ignored him.

At a press conference with Tose (left) and Retzlaff (right).

One of his defensive linemen started dating a woman who just happened to be Joe's secretary. Joe didn't find out about it until she told him she was quitting to get married.

But it was Kuharich's relationship with the public that was really sour. Because of the 15-year contract, he had an openly condescending attitude that went over like a lead balloon in the city. The fans felt Joe was extremely arrogant; when he was on radio or TV or talking to reporters, he would just antagonize the shit out of people. He couldn't help himself. It was like picking at a scab. He would say things like, "I'll be here long after you're gone." He wasn't a bad guy at all, but he had a knack for saying things that just aggravated the hell out of the fans. That's bad enough under normal circumstances, but when you're losing like we were back then, it can get pretty ugly. And we lost a lot during Joe's five years with the Eagles. He had just one winning season (9–5 in 1966) and won just two games in 1968, his last year there.

Joe and Ed Snider were at odds much of the time while Kuharich was the team's coach. Ed couldn't stand the way Joe would publicly flaunt the 15-year contract Jerry had given him. Jerry ignored it, but Ed couldn't. And Joe drove our public relations people crazy because none of the local reporters could stand him. Joe made it more difficult for our PR people to do their job because of his arrogant attitude toward the public.

In 1968 the Eagles won only two games, going 2–12. The public distaste for Joe was right out there in the open. Planes would fly over Franklin Field with Joe Must Go banners. After games, there would be a flatbed truck with a rock band on it holding a rally urging the firing of Kuharich. This went on for quite some time, until Leonard Tose— who bought the team from Wolman in 1969 for the then-record price of $15.1 million—finally fired Joe as his first official act as the new owner.

Tose brought in former Eagles tight end Pete Retzlaff to be the team's general manager and hired Jerry Williams to replace Kuharich as head coach. Joe might've been gone, but he certainly wasn't forgotten. He had 10 years left on his contract when he was fired, and Leonard was obligated to keep paying him for every one of those 10 years.

After Leonard bought the team, there was a lot of discussion about whether or not they could get out of the contract with Joe. My feeling, when Leonard would ask me, was that a deal is a deal. Jerry had given Joe the 15-year deal, and we were obligated to pay him for all 15 years. Some others in the organization, though, didn't agree with that and thought we could get out of it.

Not long after he was fired by the Eagles, Joe got very sick. He had cancer. Eagles fans hated Joe, but it still would have looked very bad for the organization if it had tried to get out of paying him the money he was owed on his contract. Joe and his family lived out on the Main Line, and I frequently delivered his checks to him personally to make sure he got them.

About a year after the last payment, Joe passed away at the age of 63. He died on January 25, 1981, which coincidentally enough was the day the Eagles lost to the Oakland Raiders in Super Bowl XV.

Later in my career, I had the pleasure of working with Joe's youngest son, Bill, during the three years I spent with the Philadelphia Stars of the United States Football League. Bill was the Stars' player personnel director and would go on to have a long and successful career in the NFL as a personnel man. He worked for the New Orleans Saints, Kansas City Chiefs, and Cleveland Browns, and was the Saints' president and general manager for several years. He and his wife, Betsy—who also worked for the Stars—are longtime friends.

After Leonard took over in 1969, his top financial guy, Sid Forstater, promoted me to both ticket manager and business manager. I was a pretty busy guy, which was fitting, because the Tose era would see the pace of the Eagles organization increase and get more frenetic.

Chapter 5

Leonard's Women

Tose, whose family owned a Philadelphia trucking company, had been one of the Happy Hundred, the investment group headed by James P. Clark that had owned the Eagles from 1949 until Wolman bought them in 1963.

As I said, the pace got faster—and crazier—during Leonard's ownership. I never met a man who was so obsessed with extravagance and personal convenience. I mean, the man would take a helicopter to work, for God's sake. Maybe that's not so unusual today, but it was back then.

He was a free-spending jet-setter, and his foolish spending would eventually catch up with him. But during much of the 15 years he owned the team, he acted like there was no bottom to his wealth. I mean, the guy had people whose job it was to open doors for him and make sure they had the right scotch at whatever gathering he attended. He paid people to do everything. He almost never had a piece of paper on his desk.

The women in Leonard's life were another story. He was the ultimate womanizer. He would pick up and go to Cannes or someplace else with one of his girlfriends at a moment's notice, and everyone else had to make the arrangements for his trips. It was a wonder he could even step on the plane by himself.

He was married and divorced four times. After he divorced his second wife, Andrea, in 1980, he took up with a woman named Betsy Rubin.

Betsy was followed by Leonard's third wife, Caroline, who was a flight attendant—they called them stewardesses back then. I believe there was a short fling with a Debbie after he divorced Caroline. We used to joke that he was trying to go through the alphabet—A, B, C, D. Somebody said that when he got to Wilhelmina, we would need to take away his vitamins.

When Leonard was married to Andrea, he put her in charge of decorating the team's offices at Veterans Stadium, which opened in 1971. Andrea hired a decorator and an architect but oversaw everything. Then, suddenly, one day there was no sign of Andrea. We had no idea what had happened to her.

A little while later, we started seeing a new woman around the office. Her name was Betsy Rubin. Betsy was married to Mickey Rubin, who was sort of the furniture king of Philadelphia at the time. Soon stories started surfacing in the gossip columns about the love triangle between Leonard and Mickey and Betsy. Leonard stole Betsy from Mickey, and Mickey was pissed.

One day when Leonard and Betsy were going hot and heavy, I was called to the ticket office lobby. We were holding a game off local TV because we hadn't sold all of the 100-level seats at Veterans Stadium. The seats weren't actually part of *our* stadium capacity. We shared the Vet with the Phillies, and those seats had been built for them; they were left over from the Phillies' season and were not on the original manifest for football.

But Leonard insisted that if those seats didn't get sold, we were going to black out the game. Eagles fans were not happy that the game possibly was going to be blacked out. It became a big story because no one felt we should be able to black out a game for not selling seats that were built for baseball.

When I got down to the ticket office lobby, there was this big guy—he was about 6'5"—standing there. His name was Herky Herkelin. Herky had played basketball at LaSalle and was a former bodybuilder, and he was very imposing. He had Tom Fox, a columnist for the *Philadelphia Daily News*, with him. It's seldom good when a 6'5" bodybuilder shows up at your doorstep. And it's even worse when he brings along a reporter.

Anyway, Herky said he was there on behalf of Mickey Rubin, handed me a blank check, and said Mickey wanted to buy all of the unsold 100-level seats that were causing the TV blackout. I looked at the check and, sure enough, it was from the Rubin Furniture Company. Herky said Mickey would sue Leonard for discrimination if he didn't accept the check.

Mickey, who had his wife stolen from him by Leonard, was going to make a promotion out of buying up all the tickets and making Leonard look bad at the same time. In his story on the whole thing the next day, Fox referred to Leonard as Old Eagle Eyebrows because Leonard always had those huge, overgrown eyebrows.

When Herkelin first gave me the check for the seats from Mickey Rubin, I was very nervous. Leonard was very good at shooting the messenger, and here I was, having to go and tell him that his girlfriend's husband—Leonard and Betsy never actually got married—was paying for the seats and that it was going to be a big story in the paper because there had been a reporter there.

Leonard was furious. I don't think I had heard that many F-sharps since the Marine Corps. He was smoking a cigarette and would rant between puffs. He told me what to tell the guy, which was to go fuck himself. Leonard said he'd rather forfeit the television revenue than let Rubin buy up the seats. So I went back to the ticket office and told Herky Herkelin there was no deal. He looked down at me—he was at least eight inches taller than me—and said, "I hear you're a good guy. You won't get hurt." To this day, I wonder if my getting hurt was ever on the agenda.

All of Philly had a good laugh at Leonard's expense over this. The headline in the *Daily News* the next day was "Carpet King Pulls the Rug Out From Under Tose." Ultimately the tickets were finally all sold, the blackout was lifted, and the game was televised locally. And Mickey

Rubin and his furniture store got more publicity than they knew what to do with—all for free. Just another day in the life of Leonard Tose.

When Leonard was married to Andrea and the office decor at the Vet was her responsibility, we needed rugs. Carpeting the Eagles' offices was no small job, and I put the rugs out for bid. There was a department store in Philly back then called Lit Brothers. They won the bid for our office rugs. The guy we dealt with was named Max. Max and Lit carpeted the whole place.

It was right after the rugs were installed that Andrea disappeared. One of the first things Betsy Rubin said when she walked into the offices was, "I hate the rugs." I immediately got a call from one of Leonard's assistants who said he needed to see me. I went into Leonard's office, and he said, "Get rid of these blankety-blank rugs." I walked out of his office in a state of astonishment and called Max over at Lit Brothers. I said, "Max, we need new rugs." This was, I kid you not, just 30 days after the original installation. Max never had a better 30-day client. All of the carpets were replaced. Max loved it.

Chapter 6

Hey, Duke, How Much You Want for Your Yacht?

As I mentioned earlier, after Leonard bought the team in May 1969, he hired Pete Retzlaff to be his general manager. Pete was a tight end for the Eagles for 10 years, from 1956 to 1966. He played on the 1960 championship team and led that team in receiving with 46 catches and 826 yards. He's in the team's Hall of Fame.

I still remember Pete's words when he became the GM. He said, "If this infant doesn't grow, I'll be the one who didn't feed it." Back then a hot topic of discussion was whether to make season-ticket holders buy tickets to exhibition games—or preseason games, as the league has long preferred to call them. After Leonard bought the team, he decided to add preseason games in the season-ticket package. To no one's surprise, the fans went absolutely nuts. They felt cheated. It's accepted as the way the NFL does business today, but back then it was a very big deal.

Leonard and Pete became very nervous about all of this. We had an emergency meeting to decide whether to keep the preseason games on the season-ticket strip. I remember sitting in Pete's office before we went out to meet the press. Pete asked me what I thought. I told him that if it were up to me, I wouldn't even address this issue with the press right now. I said we should take our time and let the anger die down and then make a decision.

But Pete didn't like the pressure. We went out and met the press, and he made the preseason games optional. Eventually every team in the NFL, including the Eagles, would add the preseason games to their season-ticket package. Fans don't like it, but they've gotten used to it.

As for the unfed child, well, that kid didn't eat very well during Pete's tenure as GM. The team was pretty lousy. Jerry Williams, who replaced Kuharich, lasted just three years as head coach. His teams went 4–9–1, 3–10–1, and 6–7–1. He was replaced by Eddie Khayat, who was fired after winning just two games in his one and only season as head coach. Next came Mike McCormack, who lasted three years and also never had a winning season. Those weren't the glory days of the Eagles, to be sure. It didn't take long for Leonard to tire of Retzlaff, and Pete left after just four years on the job.

Leonard was hoping a new stadium would help Eagles fans forget about how bad the team was. The city built Veterans Stadium, one of those multipurpose monstrosities that were so popular in the 1970s and early '80s. As I said before, it housed both the Eagles and the Phillies.

It was supposed to be completed in time for the 1970 season, but there were unexpected 11th-hour delays and we didn't end up moving in until the 1971 season. That ended up being a nightmare for me. I already had relocated all of our season-ticket holders from Franklin Field to the new facility for the 1970 season. When the city's managing director came in and told me the bad news—that we would have to play another year at Franklin Field—I had to move all of the season-ticket holders back over there.

And that wasn't all. The league schedule already had come out before we were told the opening of the Vet was going to be delayed. Our schedule included a November Monday night game against the Giants on ABC. The problem was, Franklin Field didn't have any lights.

Retzlaff, Fred Schobel (Penn's athletic director at the time), and I sat down and negotiated a deal for the installation of lights at Franklin Field so we could play the Monday night game there. Penn has played only a handful of night games there over the years; those lights mainly have been used for the school's intramural sports program. But if anybody ever asks you how Franklin Field came to have lights, you now know the answer.

That 1970 Eagles-Giants Monday night game at Franklin Field is mostly remembered for ABC broadcaster Howard Cosell getting drunk and throwing up all over the boots of his broadcast partner, "Dandy" Don Meredith. Cosell had spent several hours before the game hammering down martinis with Tose's wife. On top of that, Leonard sent champagne up to the booth during the game. Howard ultimately had to be carried out of the booth at halftime by two security guards after puking on Meredith. He never saw the second half. Cosell later explained his second-half absence from the booth as a case of the flu. Yeah, the martini and champagne flu.

Leonard had a reputation as being a kind and generous person, which, in many ways, he was. But people don't remember the other side of him, which I had the misfortune of seeing up close and personal.

One day—I can't remember which year it was—we were talking about an upcoming game. Until he hired Dick Vermeil in 1976, the Eagles were pretty bad under Leonard's stewardship. I mentioned offhandedly that our fans deserved a win, that it was time for them to taste some success. He looked at me and replied, "Fuck the fans. *I* deserve it a lot more than they do."

Another time, after we moved into the Vet, I got a call from the mayor at the time, Frank Rizzo. He wanted some tickets. I ran it by Leonard, who said, "Get them for him. Take the seats away from anyone you have to, but get those seats and give them to Frank."

I still remember the guy whose seats we took screaming about his loyalty to the team and saying he couldn't believe we could be so cruel. He was absolutely 100 percent correct. But Leonard didn't care. I always hated hurting fans, anyway. I don't pretend that I was always able to help them, but I always tried. Many times, when I had to say no back then, I was covering for the ownership.

It's been said that Leonard never had a partner who didn't end up suing him. That might be true. The first one I remember was a guy named John Connelly, who was part of the syndicate headed by Tose that bought the team from the bankrupt Wolman. Shortly after the sale, the two had a falling out. The papers were full of alleged broken promises by Leonard. Litigation followed. It was one of dozens of lawsuits Leonard was involved in over the years. Most of his original partners in the sale eventually ended up selling their shares and getting out because of him.

Leonard loved letting people know how rich and powerful he was. He had a helicopter, and he was obsessed with it. He would take it to the office every day from his home in Radnor. There was a tiny grass area right outside the stadium offices. It wasn't very big, but Leonard decided it was plenty big enough for his helicopter to land. Convenience was Leonard's middle name.

He would take the helicopter to training camp, where somebody would have to pick him up in a golf cart that had a fringe canopy that protected him from the sun. What a sight. The players used to laugh their asses off. His arrival at training camp was always a distraction. The quarterback would be calling signals, and then he would be drowned out by the sound of Leonard's helicopter.

Leonard took it to the shore and many other places. The chopper supposedly was co-owned by one of the team's minority partners, Herb Barness. I guess Herb saw the inside of it a few times but damn few. It was Leonard's baby. It ended up being one of many things that caused a rift between Leonard and Barness. Barness, who owned 29 percent of the team, offered Tose $21.5 million for the Eagles in 1977 but was turned down. Shortly after that, Barness sold his stake in the team.

Leonard was always looking for ways to flaunt his wealth, even as he was losing much of it down at the casinos in Atlantic City. And he was very, very good at it—flaunting his wealth, I mean, not gambling. He sucked at gambling.

Once, when the team was out in California, he threw a party on a yacht. He had rented a yacht, but when he found out John Wayne had a yacht nearby, he sent his errand people to find the Duke and ask him if he could use his yacht for the party instead. He got it, but hardly anyone at the party realized whose yacht it was, and he ended up spending twice as much to rent the Duke's yacht as the original yacht.

I remember going to a league event once. I can't remember if it was a Super Bowl or an owners meeting or what it was. Anyway, the league threw this huge party. Kay and I were there with a big group of Eagles people that included Leonard.

The food, which was magnificent, was served buffet style. Each table had a waiter to get drinks for people, but everybody went up to the buffet to get their own food. That included the commissioner and every other NFL owner at the party. Well, Leonard thought he was different. At one point, he turned to the waiter and said, "Aren't you going to serve us?" When the waiter told him he was just there to get the drinks, Leonard abruptly stood up and told the entire entourage, "OK, let's go. We're leaving," and stormed out of the place. The buffet was good enough for the Rooneys and the Maras and Pete Rozelle and other NFL royalty, but not for Leonard.

Kay and I decided to stay. Somebody in Leonard's entourage turned to me and said, "Well, Leo, I hope I get to eat tonight." The good news was that Kay and I suddenly had an entire table to ourselves. What a feast for a couple of North Philly kids.

I remember one time not long after Leonard bought the Eagles, the team was playing really poorly, which happened a lot back then. He decided to go down to the locker room and give them a pep talk before practice one day. During his talk, Leonard told them they should consider him their "father away from home." He said if they needed anything, like a father, he would take care of them.

Right after the meeting, one of our linebackers, Bill Hobbs, went up to Leonard and said, "Hey, Dad, I'm going out tonight. Can I borrow the car?" Well, after practice ended, there was a chauffeur-driven limousine waiting outside the stadium for Hobbs and a bunch of his buddies. Not only that, but their "father" picked up their entire tab that night. Unfortunately, it didn't help them play any better.

There are countless legendary stories about Leonard's spending. When he finally had to sell the Eagles in 1985, he was 70 years old. He lived 18 more years before dying in 2003 at the age of 88, but he spent many of those final 18 years penniless. Though he sold the team for $65 million, most of the proceeds went to banks and casinos and other people he owed money to. He would've lost the team much sooner were it not for the league. The NFL didn't want to see any team go under; it makes for really bad publicity. So it did everything it could to help Leonard. But every penny he got, he squandered.

At one point Detroit Lions owner William Ford came to his rescue with a huge loan to keep the banks at bay. As the team's business manager at the time, I had tried very hard to control expenses, but it was an uphill battle with Leonard. And when he got the new loan via Ford, I lost control. He was like a kid on Christmas morning

Former Eagles quarterback Ron Jaworski offered to help Leonard once by hosting a benefit that would've raised potentially a million dollars for Leonard. To which Leonard replied, "C'mon, Ron, I need *real* money." Even when he was broke, a million dollars was nothing to him. At one point, he even privately pawned his Super Bowl ring.

Part of Leonard's deal with Norman Braman when he sold the Eagles to him was that he receive 25 Super Bowl tickets each year. Leonard, of course, would scalp them for a very high price. He just couldn't stop spending. Sure, the gambling didn't help, but his exorbitant spending was as big a reason for his downfall as the gambling and drinking. Leonard

Late Eagles owner Leonard Tose with late NFL commish Pete Rozelle in '84 at press conference to announce that the league was going to help Tose with his money woes.

would've spent his final years homeless if not for Dick Vermeil. Dick constantly gave him money, though it never was enough for Leonard. Dick's generosity to his former boss went well into the high six figures, but Leonard managed to squander all of it.

I'll never forget the time Leonard took me to the Jersey Shore in his helicopter. Kay and the kids were already down there on vacation. I was about to drive down and meet them when Leonard told me he was headed down there too and would give me a ride. It wasn't a request; he basically ordered me to get in the helicopter.

The problem was he was going to Atlantic City and I was going to Sea Isle, which are about 30 miles apart. The pilot dropped him off in AC, where he had a limo waiting to take him to his house, where one of his many women was waiting for him. He hopped out without a word, got into the limo, and took off. Meanwhile, I was still in the helicopter with the pilot.

The pilot flew that thing like he was fresh out of Vietnam, which, as it turned out, he was. We had a great view of the whitecaps of the ocean. He headed for Sea Isle but had no idea where he was going to land. He was asking me what to do, like I did this every day. There's a saying—prior planning prevents poor performance. The pilot kept asking me for suggestions on where to land. We couldn't land on the beach with all that sand. So where did we end up picking? Would you believe a playground? That's right, a playground. I'm guessing that probably violated a few aeronautical rules, not to mention a few Sea Isle town ordinances.

There were kids on rides, and a bunch of guys were playing softball. As we got closer to the ground, nobody was moving because they were in disbelief. They obviously were thinking, *Surely he's not going to put it down on a playground, right?* Wrong.

As we got closer to the ground, it dawned on everybody that this was not a drill. Bats, balls, and gloves went flying everywhere as we touched down. The pilot said, "We used to do this in 'Nam." To which I replied, "Except we're not in 'Nam. We're in fucking Sea Isle."

I got out of there in a big hurry. But it wasn't like you couldn't tell whose helicopter it was. It was painted kelly green with a green helmet and green wings on it. Rules were not made for Leonard. Good thing there weren't iPhones back then. That landing would've gone viral, and I would've been permanently banned from setting foot in Sea Isle.

Chapter 7

Take These Seats and Shove Them Up Your Ass

I believe I'm the only ticket manager in history who has taken the same team into three different stadiums. I moved the Eagles from Franklin Field to Veterans Stadium in 1970, only to have to move them back to Franklin Field when the Vet wasn't ready for occupancy. A year later, when the Vet was finally completed, I had to move them back in there. Then in 2003 we made the move from the Vet, which we had shared with the Phillies for 31 years, to our current home, Lincoln Financial Field.

Franklin Field, which is on the University of Pennsylvania campus, was a terrific place to watch a football game. Penn's football team still plays there, and the Penn Relays are held there every spring. When I was with the Stars, we even played a playoff game at Franklin Field in 1984, beating the Donald Trump–owned New Jersey Generals.

The locker rooms at Franklin Field were terrible back when the Eagles played there. I'm sure they've had a facelift since then, but in the 1960s, they ranked near the bottom of the league. But that wasn't something that affected the fans.

Franklin Field was a horseshoe with the west end zone open. For the 1960 championship game against the Packers, we put extra seats in the west end zone. The seats there had no backs; they were just wooden benches that caused countless people to get splinters in their asses. I think it gave people a college feeling watching a pro game. When people stood up to cheer, the person on the end of the row often lost his seat when everybody sat back down. But the fans loved the place.

My game day office was in the ticket office at Penn. Back in the day, I used to carry all of our papers and records from our 30th Street office to the Franklin Field ticket office in case I needed any information. The whole setup was tedious and had many drawbacks. I would hang out on the west sideline and watch part of the game in the southwest corner of the stadium.

On that freezing cold night when we played the Monday night game at Franklin Field and Cosell got plastered, he wasn't the only one inebriated. Many of the fans were so drunk they took off their shirts and paraded around the area by the scoreboard. God, what this game does to people.

Veterans Stadium was very different. It was one of a number of multipurpose stadiums that popped up in the early 1970s in cities with professional baseball and football teams. But the Vet clearly favored the Phillies. The football playing field was a mile away from the stands. There was very little room between the back of the end zone and the wall.

On top of all that, the artificial turf at the Vet was notoriously awful. The NFL Players Association did an annual ranking of the league's most dangerous playing surfaces, and the Vet regularly had the dubious distinction of being No. 1—deservedly so. The seams and the covers for the cutouts for the baseball base areas were death traps. One year Bears wide receiver Wendell Davis shredded both of his knees when one of his cleats got caught in a seam.

We shared many things at the Vet with the Phillies, including the showers. The team eventually had to build additional offices for the coaches on the lower level because there wasn't enough room up on the third floor, where the executive offices were. As our organization grew, we put in a weight room. But it was so small, it was a miracle players didn't drop weights on one another.

Slowly but surely it became evident that we needed more space and better facilities. As time went on, the city didn't really take very good care of the Vet, and it fell into disrepair. Rats and mice were all over the place. I remember once taking the elevator down to the field level. The doors opened, and standing there right in front of me was this giant rat. I mean, it was the size of a damn cat. I was glad to get out of there.

When free agency came into being in the mid-1990s, the Vet, which also served as the team's training facility, was a real problem in convincing free agents to sign with the Eagles. Other teams had gorgeous state-of-the-art training facilities and brand-new stadiums, and we had the Vet, which leaked like a sieve and reeked of cat piss.

All that has changed now, of course. When Jeffrey Lurie bought the team from Norman Braman in 1994 and brought along his longtime friend Joe Banner to help him run it, they had a vision of what they wanted to do, and it started with a separate state-of-the-art training facility and a football-only stadium.

The training facility, which is called the NovaCare Complex, was built on the corner of Broad and Pattison in South Philadelphia, on the site of a former naval hospital. It opened in 2001. Two years later, just a quarter mile away, on the other side of Pattison Street, Lincoln Financial Field opened.

With tons of suites and club areas, terrific sight lines, and countless amenities, it's both a fan's stadium and a corporate stadium, suited to make money in many more ways than just selling seats. Besides playing our home games there, Temple also uses it for their home games. We've also hosted soccer games and major concerts and other events there. A writer for the *Daily News* once dubbed Lincoln Financial Field Cha-Ching Stadium. He was pretty accurate. It has made Jeffrey a lot of money.

But I'm getting ahead of myself. There was a time when the Vet— where a parking lot for the Eagles' and Phillies' stadiums now lies—was new as well. And though there were no rats yet, there were plenty of problems. In fact, those problems started before the Vet was even *built*.

When they were building the Vet, the city would hold regular meetings with the teams. Leonard couldn't be bothered with them. The Phillies had lawyers and accountants and architects and engineers and executives at these meetings. We had nobody. The city finally told Leonard that the Eagles needed to be represented at these meetings since they were going to be one of the two tenants.

Since I was one of the few people leftover from the Wolman era, Leonard said, "Send Leo. He's been around." Just me. Nobody else. It was a bit overwhelming but a great experience. I handled those big architectural drawings as if I knew what I was looking at.

Before I went to my first meeting of the stadium committee, I stopped by Leonard's office and asked him if he had any special instructions. He took a long drag on his cigarette and said, "Yeah. You better make sure my office is fucking bigger than this one." No instructions on anything about the fan accommodations or the concessions or the restrooms or the seating. Just the size of his new office. What a guy.

So I went to the meeting, and as it turned out, some of the office plans already had been decided on, and Leonard's office wasn't nearly big enough. I said, "For God's sake and mine, please knock these walls down surrounding Leonard's office and make it one big office." The architects were kind to me. They also knew Leonard's ego and personality. They obliged me and Leonard got his big office, though I'm sure he would have tried to raise the ceiling if there had been a way to do so.

Being on the stadium committee was only a small part of my job. I also had the huge responsibility of transferring the season-ticket holders from Franklin Field to the Vet. What a nightmare that was. We finally sent out the seat notices (with the new seat assignments), and my popularity in the city took an immediate nosedive. Moving people from a football stadium to a combination football-baseball stadium was an impossible situation in itself. Add to that the fact that Leonard insisted

I take care of hundreds of others—which included his friends, people at Tose Trucking, his neighbors in Norristown, you name it—and we had some very unhappy people on our hands.

This was another one of those situations where I had to take the hit for ownership. I didn't mind, because that's what I got paid to do. But Leonard exacerbated the difficulties of the move with his "take care of my friends first" demands.

I had to send out a form to all of his friends and associates. They would write down their "requests" and send it back to me. They could write anything they wanted on there and I was under orders to accommodate them regardless of where they wanted to sit or how many tickets they wanted.

Bottom line: fans who had been loyal season-ticket holders for years got screwed. Franklin Field and Veterans Stadium were entirely different, and even under the most ideal circumstances, it would have been a tough

The move from Franklin Field to Veterans Stadium made a lot of fans unhappy.

conversion to move people from one to the other. But when the owner had his hands in the ticket pot up to his elbows, it was next to impossible.

There were countless articles in the paper about all the unhappy fans. I was quoted several times trying to defend the transfer. But I could never tell them about that damn request form Leonard made me give to all his people.

I truly hated what was happening, hated not taking care of our own fans first. But Leonard made it clear that he and his friends always came first. It filtered down to many of his business associates as well, which ended up being more than a little ironic, as many of those associates became his enemies down the road in his numerous legal battles.

The Vet was supposed to open in time for the 1970 NFL season. I spent months moving all of our season-ticket holders out of Franklin Field and into the new multipurpose stadium. All systems were go.

Then in August, just before our first preseason game, Fred Corletto, who was the managing director of the city of Philadelphia at the time, stopped by my office. He looked at me and said, "I didn't want to tell you this over the phone, but I've got bad news. The stadium's not going to be ready."

I almost fainted. It was just a week before the start of the season and we had to move back to Franklin Field and give everybody their old seats back for the 1970 season. There were no computers back then; we had to do it all manually. With time a seemingly insurmountable issue, I hired a number of people from local theaters and other venues to help me put everybody back in Franklin Field. Even my wife, Kay, would get a babysitter and come down to the Eagles offices and help. One girl I hired took so much flak over the phone that she threw the phone down and walked out, never to be seen or heard from again. During this time, one reporter wrote a story calling me "the toughest Eagle of them all." I loved it. At the time, maybe I was. If I got three hours of sleep that week, it was a lot.

Against all odds, we moved everybody back to Franklin Field, and then we had the whole painful process of moving everybody back to the Vet again a year later to look forward to. Needless to say, those were trying times for this former altar boy.

It was next to impossible to make everybody happy when we finally moved from Franklin Field to the Vet for the 1971 season, especially with Leonard hoarding tickets for all of his friends. I'll never forget, shortly after we had made the move and I ran into this guy on the elevator. He was carrying something heavy and I asked him if he needed help with it. He looked at me and said, "No, I have it."

I said, "Welcome to the stadium. My name's Leo Carlin and I work for the Eagles."

He said, "I know who you are."

I said, "Oh, OK. Well, is there anything I can do for you?"

"No," he said in a surly voice. Then he stepped off the elevator, turned to me, and said, "Actually there is something you can do for me. You can take these seats you gave me and shove them up your fucking ass." I guess you can't please everybody.

I still remember our first game at the Vet after we finally moved in. It was a preseason game against the Buffalo Bills. It seemed like everybody in the city wanted to be there for that first game, even though it was a meaningless exhibition game.

There was a platform outside the stadium club from which you could see the people arriving. People were actually climbing the walls to get in because the game was sold out. Traffic was backed up for miles. The fans stuck their fingers through the steel mesh of the fence and stormed the stadium. I stood there with Leonard and Pete Retzlaff and watched it all in disbelief. There was nothing anyone could do. I went on the radio and told people to turn around and go home and watch the game on TV. Rarely do you tell fans not to come to a game. But in this case, it was necessary. It was a scary situation. Fortunately, no one was seriously hurt.

As it turned out, because of my involvement with the stadium construction, I ended up developing a strong association and many great relationships with the Phillies. Years later, when the both of us were moving out of Veterans Stadium and into new stadiums—the Eagles into Lincoln Financial Field and the Phillies into Citizens Bank Park across the street—they had a countdown of the games they had left at the Vet, and they let me take a number down off the outfield wall before one of the games.

Some great people were given the honor of participating in the countdown, including Harry Kalas, Tug McGraw, and many others. I can't tell you how blown away I was that they asked me do it.

I was to be driven out onto the field by the Phillie Phanatic. I had forgotten that the Phanatic was Tom Burgoyne. Burgoyne replaced the original Phanatic, Dave Raymond, back in 1993 and was a former high school classmate of my son Clayton. While we were waiting to drive

Riding shotgun with the Philly Phanatic.

out onto the field, his big nose turned toward me and he said, "Hi, Mr. Carlin. How's Clayton doing?"

Before Tom took me onto the field, I was thinking to myself that I could get a pretty bad reception since we had just mailed out the notices for the season-ticket holders' seat locations for Lincoln Financial Field. I waved to the crowd as Tom drove me around the field, and much to my relief, the fans gave me a nice ovation. It was a big thrill. I got to take down the No. 28. The Phillies even framed the number and gave it to me. It was something I'll never forget, and it most likely would not have occurred had Leonard not assigned me to be on the Vet's stadium committee all those years before.

Back in the day, I used to speak at banquets. My unique experience at moving the Eagles from Franklin Field to Veterans Stadium and back to Franklin Field and back to Veterans Stadium again and then to Lincoln Financial Field provided me with a lot of great material. I used to include some of it in a David Letterman–like Top 10 list routine. The topic: why I have to get a different seat from the one you gave me. Here's a sample:

10. "I can't catch a field goal because you sat me with animals."
9. "I should get a better seat because I gave up going to my daughter's christening to go to an Eagles game."
8. "The people behind me won't go to the restroom and are peeing in a cup."
7. "I want to be near the tunnel so I can see the players sweat coming out of the locker room."
6. "I want to be near the other tunnel so I can see the cheerleaders sweat coming out of their locker room."
5. "I deserve a better seat because I buried my father in an Eagles jersey."
4. "I have to be moved because you have me sitting next to my ex-wife and her new boyfriend."
3. "My father—who has arthritis, emphysema, a bad back, and an artificial knee, and is on oxygen—is with me."

2. "I'm over 80 years old. The colostomy failed. I wear diapers and I can't make it to the men's room."

And the No. 1 reason why I need a different seat from the one you gave me: "When we moved from Franklin Field to Veterans Stadium, you really screwed me. And sure enough, you did it again."

Most of these I didn't make up. Honest to God. I had a guy call me once to complain about where we put him. He said he'd call me back later because he was at his mother's funeral. Can you imagine that?

Chapter 8
The Move to the Linc

When we were moving from the Vet to the Linc in 2003, I was pretty popular in town. Everybody wanted to get the best spot possible in the new stadium. I used to get tons of calls. Our switchboard and IT people used to count the number of callers who were trying to get to my extension. They estimated it came to 2,000 a week. I tried to answer as many as I could, but I missed a few.

I'm very proud of how the transfer from the Vet to the Linc went. Other teams that moved to new stadiums had many more problems with their season-ticket holders than we did. Yeah, we had a few unhappy people, some threats of litigation. But all in all, most of the fans were fairly happy with where they ended up when we moved them to the new stadium in '03. No transfer is ever going to be perfect and smooth, but I think we caught a lot less flak than most teams did, certainly much less than when we moved from Franklin Field to the Vet.

Still, getting to that point took a lot of doing, and the move from Veterans Stadium to Lincoln Financial Field was the most difficult of all the moves I took part in over the years. We had to deal with seat licenses and somehow try to fit everyone into the new stadium, even though the capacity for the regular seats was smaller than at the Vet.

Lincoln Financial Field's capacity is 69,000, which is actually about 4,000 more than the Vet. But it has double the amount of luxury-type seating—luxury boxes, club seating, etc.—and wheelchair-accessible seats, all of which reduced the number of regular seats we could assign to season-ticket holders. We also held some of the better seats for friends, associates, and our marketing partners at the expense of our season-ticket holders.

Let me make this clear: I'm not suggesting that the demands made by the current ownership on me going into Lincoln Financial Field were nearly as bad as what happened under Leonard when we moved to Veterans Stadium. Jeffrey was very fair with the public. Marketing, sponsorships, business relationships, and the like are just a reality of sports today.

Of the 69,000 seats at the Linc, 29,000 included a Stadium Builder License (SBL), which was a onetime fee you had to pay in addition to the cost of your season ticket. The 29,000 seats with SBLs all were either in the lower bowl of the stadium or the loge level—basically the best seats in the house.

SBLs have become pretty commonplace in stadium construction; many teams affix them to nearly all of their seats. But we did it with just a little more than 40 percent of our seats. But there still was a lot of complaining from season-ticket holders about the whole thing, and understandably so—the inclusion of the SBL brought each season-ticket price to $800!

I never thought I would see the day when a seat for a football game would cost $800. In the Eagles' first season in 1933, you could buy a ticket to a game at Municipal Stadium for 75 cents. A ticket to the 1960 NFL Championship Game at Franklin Field between the Eagles and the Green Bay Packers could be had for $8.

We also used to run great promotions that kept prices down. Years ago we had a ticket program called the father-and-son ticket. It was basically a two-for-one deal. A father could bring his son for free. If the ticket cost was $10, the father and son could both watch the game for $10. It was very popular, but not surprisingly, many people tried to take advantage of

Rappelling down Lincoln Financial Field not long after its opening in 2003.

it. I remember this one instance where the "father" was 32 and the "son" looked to be about 28. We eventually stopped that program.

Of course, you get a few other amenities for your money today, such as a pregame brunch or an on-field pregame sideline pass, which people love. Also the $800 seats were right on the 50-yard line and were held back for VIPs and special promotions, such as the Touchdown Club, which was a $750-a-seat deal.

We limited SBLs to only 29,000 seats as part of the agreement the team made with the city and then-mayor Ed Rendell when the city and state agreed to fund two-thirds of the $360 million construction cost of the stadium. That $360 million is chump change compared to the *$5 billion* construction price for the Los Angeles Rams' new stadium complex, which will open this season.

Between 1995 and 2003, 18 of the league's 32 teams either built new stadiums or did major renovations to their existing stadiums. The list includes St. Louis (1995, a lot of good that did them), Jacksonville (1995), Carolina (1996), Baltimore (1996), Washington (1997), Tampa Bay (1998), Tennessee (1999), Cleveland (1999), Cincinnati (2000), Denver (2001), Pittsburgh (2001), New England (2002), Seattle (2002), Houston (2002), Detroit (2002), Philadelphia (2003), Green Bay (2003), and Chicago (2003). The last two were only renovations, but extensive ones.

The new stadiums have been cash cows for the teams and their owners, and the Linc is no exception. It has nearly 200 luxury suites and thousands of premium seats, all of which generate a ton of money. And that doesn't even take into account the naming rights.

The Lincoln Financial Group (LFG), which is a Philadelphia-based insurance and asset-management firm, bought the naming rights to the Linc in June 2002. LFG agreed to pay $139.6 million over 21 years, or $6.65 million per year. In May 2019 they extended their deal, agreeing to pay another $167 million over the next 14 years after the initial contract expires in 2022. That's nearly $12 million in annual revenue for the

Eagles before they ever sell a ticket or a beer or a parking space, or collect their regular cut of the NFL's TV deal.

I still remember the 2002 press conference to announce that LFG had bought the naming rights to the stadium. The LFG executive at the event made a big deal of asking the media not to refer to the stadium as the Linc. They did that for obvious reasons—they wanted to get maximum publicity for their company by using the non-truncated name. But telling the media not to do something is like telling a two-year-old not to touch the fine china. Every media outlet in the city immediately began referring to the stadium as the Linc.

The Linc is a terrific place to watch a game, whether you're in one of the luxury suites or in the stands. In 2013, just 10 years after it opened the stadium, the Eagles spent $125 million on major upgrades to the place. The upgrades included seating expansion, two new HD video boards, upgraded amenities, Wi-Fi, and two new connecting bridges for the upper levels.

Good thing Leonard wasn't able to build a place like the Linc when he owned the team. That would've just been more money he would've handed over to the Atlantic City casinos.

Chapter 9
Runt of the Litter

I was born the youngest of five children. I had two sisters—Ann and Elizabeth—and two brothers: Lex (who we called Bud) and Joe. Ann passed away in 2018. Elizabeth, who we called Sis, passed away in 2020 at the age of 94. Even to her last days, she wanted to join the American Academy of Dramatic Arts and become an actress.

I couldn't hold a candle to my brothers. Since as long as I can remember, I always wanted to be like them. They were my heroes. I was 12 years younger than Lex and 13 years younger than Joe. Though Lex was a year older than Joe, he had scarlet fever when he was in first grade and was held back a year, so they ended up in the same grade and graduated high school together. As soon as they graduated in 1943, they walked out the door with the war going on and enlisted in the marines.

Imagine what that was like for my parents. I was still a little kid at the time, no more than seven. But I remember my mom was a basket case. My parents fell on the couch in our North Philly home after my brothers left and cried and cried, not knowing whether they would ever see either one of their older sons again.

Thankfully, both Lex and Joe made it back in one piece from the war. A few years later, both of them got called back to serve in the Korean War. Fortunately, they had good duty there. Bud ended up being a chaplain's assistant, and when the priest found out he had another brother in Korea

I worshipped my older brothers. Taking them to the Marine Corps Museum in Quantico in 2008 was something I'll never forget. My marine buddy Jerry St. John also joined us on the trip.

who was Catholic, he told him to go get him. So Bud and Joe both spent their two years in Korea as the chaplain's assistants and once again came back safe and sound.

I have a dollar bill at home in a frame on the wall of our family room. It's more than 75 years old. My brother Joe sent it to me on my birthday when he was stationed in New Guinea during World War II. He wrote, "Dear Kid"—that's what he used to call me—"Here's a dollar for you to spend. I know it's pretty dirty, so ask Dad if he'll give you another one that's nice and clean."

Joe was a brain, really smart. It was hard to picture him being a marine, but he was a good one. Bud was a sergeant. They inspired me to join the marines after I graduated from St. Joe's College, now St. Joe's University, in 1959.

One of the most gratifying things I've done in my life happened years later, around 2008. I took Kay and my brothers and their wives down to the National Museum of the Marine Corps outside Quantico, Virginia. Both Bud and Joe were already in their eighties. Bud's health was starting to slide; he was having trouble deciphering some things and ended up dying shortly after that. I remember as we were touring the museum, Bud was holding my hand and kept saying, "I love it! I love it! Do you hear me? I love it!" I took them to the restaurant at the Marine Corps museum down there. Afterward, both my brothers hugged me and held on to me. It was something I'll never forget.

I mentioned earlier that the Carlins had a monopoly on the entertainment industry in Philadelphia at one time: Bud ran the Forrest Theater for a long time, Joe managed the Walnut Theater, my dad ran the Apollo Theater in Atlantic City for a few years, and I worked for the Eagles.

The Apollo Theater began as a legitimate theatre. Helen Hayes performed in *Clarence* and *The Golden Age* there. The front door was located on South New York Avenue, but the side ran along Atlantic City's world-famous boardwalk. It eventually was converted to a movie theater and, like a lot of Atlantic City, fell into disrepair. It closed and was demolished in the 1970s.

I worked for my brother Bud at the Walnut Theater before I went to work full-time for the Eagles. He was upset at first when I took the job with the Eagles; he didn't understand why I wanted to get into sports. But all in all, it worked out pretty well for me.

Chapter 10

Kay, the Light of My Life

Kay and I grew up two subway stops apart in North Philly. My parish, St. Stephen's, was at Broad and Erie. She was from St. Columba's, which was at 22nd and Lehigh. Her house was just a block from Shibe Park.

I met her on a blind date. One of my best friends arranged it. That was back in 1957. I was attending St. Joe's College, and she was in nursing school. We became college sweethearts and got married two years later, on December 26, 1959.

I almost missed our wedding. A couple months after I graduated from St. Joe's, I joined the marines. I wanted to follow in my brothers' footsteps and serve my country. Even though there wasn't a war going on when I joined, my mother and father still were nervous wrecks when I left for basic training, just like they had been when Bud and Joe left for World War II and again for the Korean War.

As it turned out, my stint in the marines didn't last very long. I enlisted in Officer Candidate School after joining. I remember this sergeant we had in training. He was screaming at us and telling us how much he hated us "goddamn college kids." He used to tell us he'd shoot us in the back before he'd let any of us lead him into battle. I guess when you're a sergeant, you have to act that way.

Anyway, about four months in, they discovered I had a long-named spinal condition called spondylolisthesis; it's basically a misplaced vertebra

A photo of 2nd Platoon Charlie Company. That's me in the second row, far right.

in one's back. I knew I had it, but it wasn't a big deal and had never held me back from doing anything. But I intentionally didn't let the doctors know about it when I enlisted because I wanted badly to follow my brothers and become a marine. But at some point, the marines gave us a questionnaire that included a question about whether we had ever worn a brace. I figured the question was innocent enough, so I answered it honestly and wrote yes. A few weeks later, I got called in by the navy doctors, and they wanted to know why I had worn the brace.

As soon as I told them, I knew they weren't going to let me stay. Even back in those days, they were worried about lawsuits. I offered to sign a waiver, but that wasn't allowed. Still, it took a while for the paperwork to get processed for my discharge, which was how I almost missed our wedding.

We were supposed to get married on December 26, 1959. As the date got closer, I kept asking about the paperwork for my discharge. Every time I asked, they would tell me the same damn thing: "Don't you know that if the United States Marine Corps wanted you to have a wife, they would have issued you one with your rifle?" Ha ha.

The person who finally got it moving and enabled me to get back to Philly for my wedding was my brother-in-law. He was a dentist in the navy at the time. When I told him about my problem, he said he was going to put his uniform on and see if he could help. I wasn't sure what that meant, but he came down to the base at Quantico. I had to show him how to put on a tie and how to salute prior to his meeting with the people who were responsible for moving—or not moving—my paperwork along. I told him, "This is the United States Marine Corps. They're going to salute you. You're not drilling teeth."

So he walked into this office and said, "Sergeant, may I speak with you?" He said, "I'm interested in this particular person's papers and whether they're moving them along." Amazingly, it worked. The paperwork went through and I got discharged three days before my wedding. Otherwise, I would have been married by proxy.

My too-short time in the marines is one of the great regrets of my life. But the truth is, even as brief as it was, I wouldn't trade that experience with the 2nd Platoon Charlie Company for anything. There were 45 guys in our platoon; 33 of us still keep in touch. One of the guys in the platoon, Jerry St. John, handles the communications. When he sends out the emails, every now and then there will be another name missing, meaning someone has passed away. That's tough.

Kay and I celebrated our 60th wedding anniversary in December 2019. As I mentioned earlier, we have seven children. They came early and often. When we went out, people would stare at us, and people who knew us would see Kay and say, "My God, she's pregnant again." Kay had been a nurse, but as our family started to grow, the bulk of the

Kay and I have been married for more than 60 years.

responsibility for raising our children fell on her, so she quit nursing. I can't say enough about the exceptional job she did with them.

I love my wife dearly. She is the light of my life. But like a lot of husbands, I've been guilty of forgetting about special occasions every now and then. Valentine's Day has always given me trouble in that regard. I don't know what it is; it just seems to creep up on me.

One year I was at work, and it was about six o'clock. I was about to head home, when I realized it was Valentine's Day. I had nothing—no card, no flowers, absolutely nothing. Joe Woolley, who was our head of player personnel at the time, had received a batch of flowers from his wife earlier in the day and had them on his desk. I told Ron Howard, who was our public relations director at the time, that I was going to go back to Joe's office and grab one of the flowers, slap it in a card, and give it to

Kay, then try to get something better later. Ron thought that was a great idea. He was in the same boat, so we each took a flower. Joe's wife had sent him a dozen roses, but he still ended up with 10, and it would keep us out of hot water.

One year later, Valentine's Day came around again. It was 6:00, and again I had nothing. It was the same story with Ron again too. I went back to him and told him I was going to ask Woolley if I could steal

Kay and I cut a rug at an event in the early 2000s.

another flower from him. He said, "Uh, I wouldn't do that if I were you." I asked him why, and he said, "Well, she left him last week." So much for that.

I went to this place that sold flowers on the way home, but they were completely out. So I bought a vase and gave it to Kay. I'd pull the vase out every year. You gotta do what you gotta do.

After Kay gave birth to our seventh child, Carrie, she had a hysterectomy. That went fine, but later on she needed some follow-up surgery. During the procedure, the tape from the first surgery apparently popped out. The doctor took it and pushed it back in. As it turned out, the tape was contaminated. The result: Kay suffered an infection that has been floating around in her body for the last 22 years. No amount of antibiotics has been able to get it out. She starts getting pain, then she gets another infection. It kills me to watch her suffer and not be able to enjoy life the way she deserves to.

We could have sued the doctor and the hospital for what happened to her, but we chose not to. Kay's been to a dozen different doctors over the

Kay and I in 2012 at my Eagles Hall of Fame induction.

years and has had 22 surgeries in the last 22 years. It's a lot more than one person should have to endure. Despite all those surgeries, they haven't been able to get the infection out of her body. It's a tough scene. She's been through absolute hell for a long time.

It's been very difficult for her. She always was a vibrant woman, but that damn infection has wreaked havoc with her quality of life. She's been in and out of the hospital. Kay is a devout Catholic. Her situation would prompt a lot of people to question their faith in God, but not Kay. She turns on the TV every morning and finds a channel where she can watch Mass. I pretty much go to Mass every day also.

Chapter 11

The Dog Just Shit on Your Mother

I'm a very lucky man. I've been married to the most wonderful woman in the world for the last 60 years. We've been blessed with seven terrific kids who have given us 22 grandchildren. My life hasn't been boring. I've always said to people, if you ever get the urge to invite me out to dinner, don't ever say, "Bring your family, Leo," because there are 38 of us. We had a picture taken four Christmases ago of the entire brood; it's on the mantel of our fireplace at home.

Kay has stuck with me through thick and thin. There have been some long nights and long days, but she's always been there for me and I've always been there for her. We've been very fortunate.

After we got married, I had no clue what I was going to do. We had no place to live. You have extra guts when you're young. But everything worked out. Our first house was a little twin in Narberth. Kay spent much of the early years of our marriage pregnant; we had our first five kids in the first seven years we were married. Needless to say, we didn't live in that little twin in Narberth for very long. We had to find something bigger to house our growing family.

I think back to those days and wonder, *God in heaven, how did we ever get through that?* We didn't plan anything. The babies just kept coming

Beautiful Kay.

and coming. Yeah, like I said, we're Catholic. So much for the rhythm method.

After we were married, I got a job as the box-office manager—they called them treasurers back in those days—at the Walnut Street Theater. Several months later, the Eagles were looking for somebody to help distribute tickets. I ended up getting a part-time job in their ticket office. For the first couple years, my work was divided into seasons. There would be the theater season, where I would work at the Walnut Street Theater, and then the football season with the Eagles. Thankfully, they didn't conflict. Next to Kay and my family, football and the theater have been the two major loves of my life. I'm a big theater guy; I love the theater. We go to plays as often as possible.

On occasion, I was able to mix my theater knowledge with my job with the Eagles. Back in the days when we had to call the NFL office in New York the Thursday before home games and let them know whether the game was going to be blacked out locally, I would be the one to make that call. Usually the same woman—Nancy Behar, who would become the director of broadcast administration for the NFL—would answer the phone. Basically, all I had to do was tell her how many unsold tickets were left and whether the local network affiliate was going to be buying them. But that was too easy. I always would sing a song from a Broadway show to her. I wouldn't tell her whether the game was sold out until she guessed which show the song was from.

The Walnut Street Theater had a back door to its ticket office. One day I was on the phone, and who walks in but Henry Fonda. He got upset that I made him wait a couple minutes while I finished my phone call. At one point, he yelled out, "How in the hell are you going to sell any tickets when you're on the phone?" I told him I was on the phone with his daughter Jane trying to help her out with tickets. Jane was much nicer than her father when she came to pick up her tickets.

Besides my part-time gigs at the Walnut Street Theater and with the Eagles, I would also get what they called "spot" jobs. I would work events such as the flower show at Convention Hall. I'd be in one of those booths selling general admission tickets to people coming in. Early on, with so many mouths to feed, I would do those kinds of things on the side to make an extra buck here and there.

As I said, Kay worked as a nurse after we got married, but then the kids started to come and she had to stay home and take care of our ever-expanding family. She did a magnificent job of raising our children; I'm talking Hall of Fame–worthy. Every now and then, as they got older, one of our sons would get into an argument with her, as sons and mothers are prone to do. I remember my son Chris would say, "You're relentless, Mother. You're relentless. You're the Ronnie Lott of mothers." That became a fixture in our house. For my wife's 65th birthday, I got Lott— one of the greatest football players of all time—to make a tape for me.

Laurence and I take in a game at the Vet.

Me with my seven children. Front row (l to r): Carrie, Corinne, and Lizanne. Back row (l to r): Leo Jr., Laurence, the old man, Clayton, and Chris.

On it, he said, "Kay, you're relentless. Happy birthday." The whole family loved it.

This is a good time to tell you about our children. For starters, every one of their names begins with either an *L* or a *C*. You want to know how smart we are? We didn't realize that until after we had the fifth one. Seriously. Somebody else pointed it out to us.

Our firstborn is Lizanne, who was born only 11 months after Kay and I got married. Lizanne and her husband, Bob, who live in Drexel Hill, have done a wonderful job of raising their two children, Elissa and RJ. Elissa is a nurse. RJ recently graduated from the University of Scranton and is an accountant.

Leo came next, the first of our four boys. All of them played football in college. Leo was one of those Cinderella guys, even in college. He was a walk-on wide receiver at Holy Cross; he earned a scholarship and became their leading receiver. He got into the insurance field after he got

Kay and I decked out in our Holy Cross gear to cheer on Leo Jr.

out of college and has been very successful. He was a minority owner of the Philadelphia Soul of the Arena Football League when Jon Bon Jovi owned them along with former Eagles quarterback Ron Jaworski, who is a longtime friend.

All of our kids have different personalities. Leo is the rock. He is a stalwart. Not that the others aren't strong; they are. But he's the rock. He's a guy you can go to. I was on the phone the other day about something from years ago. Somebody wanted to have a meeting with me. I was telling Leo about it, and he said, "I'll go to that meeting with you because I don't want anybody messing around with you."

Leo and his wife, Suzanne, have four children—two boys and two girls. The boys are Keenan and Leo; the girls are Karleigh and Margo. All of them are terrific kids. Quite often, when the family is together, there are three Leos in the same room, which can be a little bit confusing.

Our third child is Clayton. Like all four of our sons, he went to St. Joe's Prep. One of his good friends and football teammates there was Rich Gannon. After he graduated from the Prep, Clayton went to Juniata, where he played football.

And he didn't leave the game behind after he graduated. Clayton is now a football coach; he's the defensive coordinator at Sam Houston State University down in Huntsville, Texas. Before that, he coached at Coastal Carolina, Bucknell, Cornell, Nebraska, New Mexico State, Villanova, and the University of Buffalo. He and his wife, Kathleen, have moved a lot.

The thing about Clayton is he is a very nice person. Not that he can't yell now and then, but he's a very good person. He cares about you; he handles people very well. You don't hear that too much about coaches.

I'm very proud of Clayton, but I have to confess that I hate that he's a coach. It's such a tough, tough life. Somebody once told me that football is a fantastic game but it's a lousy business. They were right. I remember when he told me he wanted to get into coaching, he started out by saying, "Dad, I know you don't like it, but I really want to coach." He was right: I didn't like it. But he was determined to do it.

A 2010 shot of the Leo Club: Leo Jr., Leo III, and me.

Four of my 22 grandsons meet the coach. From left to right, Isaac and Keenan, Dick Vermeil, me, and Leo III and R.J.

Clayton and Kathleen have six kids—Carson, Julia, Clayton, Brady, Cole, and Connor. Kathleen is an all-American wife and mother; she's unbelievable. Being the wife of a football coach is a thousand times tougher than being a football coach. Especially when you're raising six children.

Corinne is our middle child. The thing about Corinne is, well, she's not a football fan. In fact, she hates the game. I mean, she *really* hates it. It probably has to do with the fact that all of the boys played it and she had to constantly accommodate their workouts and game schedules growing up. There were always sweaty jocks and T-shirts lying around, and it used to absolutely drive her crazy.

Corinne would come home from school and say, "Mom, what time is dinner?" And Kay would say, "We have to wait a while. The boys are still lifting." That would always set Corinne off. She would get so mad.

She would scream and say, "I'm sick of lifting! I'm sick of football! I have a schedule too!"

Corinne and her husband, Cliff, have two children—a son, Isaac, and a daughter, Naomi. We love Cliff like a son and adore Isaac and Naomi. Ever since Isaac was born, Corinne has told us, "My boy never, ever will play football." That makes us no less proud of him or his sister. Instead of cheering them on at football games, we are their biggest fans at school plays, graduations, and other life events. We spend a lot of time with all of them during holidays, beach vacations, and family dinners.

Naomi recently graduated from high school. Not long before, we were all together talking about it, and for some reason I remembered Dick Vermeil was having his annual golf outing in a few weeks. I wasn't sure whether it was the same day as Naomi's graduation. That's all I would have had to do is tell Corinne I was going to miss Naomi's graduation for something football-related. There would've been hell to pay. I ran downstairs and checked my calendar, and thank God, there was no conflict.

Cliff comes from a strong Jewish tradition. After Naomi was born, Corinne converted to Judaism. I was an altar boy way back when and still go to church every morning. I still can recite the entire Mass for you in Latin because the nuns pounded it into my head growing up. But we didn't try to dissuade Corinne from switching religions. I guess it was something we thought about for a minute, but it would've been ridiculous. We can each take our own path in life. We share all of the holidays with them—Passover, Easter, Christmas, and Hanukkah. It was a big thrill to attend Naomi's bat mitzvah and Isaac's bar mitzvah and get called to the Torah for a blessing.

I'm not spilling secrets here by pointing out that there aren't many Jewish players in the NFL. After the Arizona Cardinals took Josh Rosen in the first round of the 2018 draft, I called Corinne and said, "Guess what. The Cardinals just drafted a Jewish kid named Rosen." The girl who hates football quickly responded, "He's only half Jewish. The other half never would have let him do it."

I remember talking to Eddie Snider one day before he died. He jokingly said to me, "You're not a big deal. I have 15 grandchildren." I said, "That's wonderful, Eddie. I have 22. But I can lend you two." He said, "What are you talking about?" I said, "Well, Corinne converted to Judaism. My grandson just had his bar mitzvah and was up on the bimah reading from the Torah."

As I mentioned, I was an altar boy growing up. The bishop was assigned to our parish, which meant there was extra Latin when he had a Mass. If they held a Latin quiz, I'd win it. Not so much with the Torah. But I am so proud of Isaac and Naomi for memorizing all of that Hebrew.

Anyway, back to the Carlin clan. Christopher is our fifth child. He's the biggest of the bunch. He played nose guard at Fordham and weighed about 230 pounds during his playing days.

He is incredibly entertaining; he is so much fun and always makes me laugh. Christopher lives in North Jersey and is in finance. He's happily married and has three teenage children. He was the one who (probably) was conceived at the Ivanhoe Hotel in Miami Beach. I'm not sure if we ever told him that story. If he reads this book, I guess he'll find out.

After Chris, we had Laurence. Laurence is a tenured professor at the University of Wisconsin–Oshkosh. He's the dean of the honors program there. Every year, he takes a group of students over to England and teaches at Cambridge. You would never figure a football family like ours would produce a philosophy professor.

I didn't see that coming his first year at Franklin & Marshall, when he was a kicker on the football team and got placed on academic probation. But then this one teacher, a philosophy professor, talked to him and gave him some advice. The very next semester, Laurence was on the dean's list. He initially majored in accounting but switched to philosophy.

Laurence and his wife have three kids. One plays football. He's the fastest kid on the team, which I never was. Another of their sons is a very good wrestler.

I enjoy visiting them, but we don't get to see them a lot because of Kay's health. She regrets that very much.

Last but certainly not least is our youngest child, Carrie. She graduated from Lafayette College and worked in the pharmaceutical industry for many years. Carrie and her husband, Michael, have two children, Gavin and Gabe. They're both beautiful boys who are sweet, energetic, and handsome. We are grateful to be able to spend a lot of time with them. One of our favorite traditions is attending the Devon Horse Show with them every year. I have no idea what's going on, but I pet the horses like a little kid.

The thing about raising seven kids is that there was never a dull moment. It wasn't easy, but I wouldn't trade it for the world. I'll never forget one of our annual summer trips to the shore. Kay and me, the kids, Kay's mother, some friends, and—oh, yeah—our dog packed into two cars, with a doghouse and the luggage strapped to the roofs.

My mother-in-law was in the backseat of the car I was driving, along with the dog. At one point, she said to me, "Leo, I think the dog needs to go out." I said, "We can't stop right now. We're on the freeway, and he's trained. He can wait a little while." Well, we went a few more miles, and once again, my mother-in-law said in a little bit more desperate tone, "Leo, I think you really ought to do something. The dog is pacing back here." To which I replied, "You have nothing to worry about. He's a great, great dog. He knows better than to go to the bathroom in the car." At precisely that moment, this beautiful animal put his paws on the side window and proceeded to take a shit all over my mother-in-law. Needless to say, I pulled over. My mother-in-law was a mess.

Kay was in the car behind us. Leo was driving. As I pulled over, they pulled up alongside us. Kay rolled down her window and asked in a calm, pleasant voice, "What's the matter?" I replied simply, "Oh, the dog just shit on your mother." I thought Leo was going to drive into the woods he was laughing so hard.

When you have a big family, there's no telling from moment to moment what's going to happen. I mean, how many guys do you know who would love it if their dog shit on their mother-in-law? By the way, it wasn't long after that that she moved in with us. So she got the last laugh.

Chapter 12
A Difficult Time

In 1969, before we moved into Veterans Stadium, we hired Jim Murray. Jim was in his mid-thirties at the time. He had been the sports information director at Villanova before he joined the organization; he bled 'Nova blue. He was funny and engaging and good with people.

Jim Murray initially worked for my good friend Jim Gallagher in our public relations department. Kay and I had Jim and his wife over for dinner shortly after he started working for the Eagles, along with Jimmy Gal and his wife, Betty. Gallagher, who passed away a couple years ago, spent 46 years with the Eagles. During the course of those 46 years, he held just about every job in the organization, including personnel director, public relations director and marketing director. He was a good, good man.

Shortly after Jim Murray started, while he was working for Jimmy Gal, Pete Retzlaff decided he needed an administrative assistant. I was asked to help with the search. I remember Pete showing me how busy he was by holding a few unanswered messages in his hand. I thought he was overreacting. I mean, there might've been 9 or 10 messages in his hand, which was nothing compared to the number of messages I would get during the course of a workday.

We had some very capable candidates for the position, including Jim Heffernan, who had previously worked for us before moving to the

81

league office, where he eventually became the NFL's top PR guy. When Jim Murray learned that Pete was looking for an administrative assistant, he came into my office and asked me if he could be considered for the job. I was thrilled. I went to Pete and told him, and Jim started working for him almost immediately.

During the brief time Jim worked for Retzlaff, he grew very close with team owner Leonard Tose. Jim ended up becoming the son that Leonard never had. He made sure that everything Leonard needed or wanted was right there at his fingertips. Leonard and Jim went on trips together, went to the racetrack together. They would sit in Leonard's office watching daytime TV. Jim made sure Leonard had the right everything at his disposal—scotch, food, you name it. They became very close. Leonard even gave Jim 1 percent of the team at one point. Their relationship was impenetrable. Like I said, Jim became the son Leonard never had.

In 1974, after a game—I can't remember which one, or even whether we won or lost—Mike McCormack held his usual postgame press conference. After he was done, Leonard stood up and said he had an announcement to make: he was making Jim Murray the team's general manager. The place was in shock. Tom Brookshier, the former Eagles great who became a broadcaster for CBS after his football career ended, told me McCormack's knuckles went white. Mike wanted the GM job but was told there never would be a GM as long as he was the coach. Retzlaff had left the organization in '72, the year before McCormack became the head coach.

The promotion clearly didn't come as a surprise to Murray. He was wearing a blue pinstripe three-piece suit. He never dressed like that. We used to kid him about the clothes he wore—yellow blazers and stuff like that.

One day Jim came to me and told me he was going to be letting "Moose" Detty go. Moose, who had been the team's longtime trainer, had spent the previous few years handling team travel. I asked Jim why he was getting rid of Moose. He told me it was to save money. Leonard

Jim Murray (left) with Tose and Dick Vermeil after the Eagles beat Dallas in the 1980 NFC Championship Game and punched their ticket to Super Bowl XV.

was spending money all over the place, and Moose—who was in poor health—became a casualty of that reckless spending.

But after letting Moose go, Jim turned around and replaced him with a close personal friend of his from Villanova, at a salary that was significantly higher than Moose's. So they didn't really save any money at all by putting Moose out on the street.

Murray stacked the front office with his pals from Villanova. Don't get me wrong; I love Villanova. I pull for them in basketball. Jay Wright, the Wildcats' basketball coach, was an intern of mine with the Stars when he first got out of Bucknell in the early 1980s. My son Clayton coached at Villanova for Andy Talley. But Jim's love for Villanova was so obvious that people used to call him Jim V.

One day at training camp, even the media got into the act. There were signs on the tables in the cafeteria at Widener University, where we trained back then, so you knew where to sit. There were tables for players, coaches, front-office staff, and the media. A couple of reporters put a Villanova sign on a couple tables because there were so many people in the organization with Villanova ties.

The team was in such financial distress during this period that the banks took over running the Eagles in order to protect their loan. They signed the checks and approved the payables. First Pennsylvania Bank was running the finances of the club under the supervision of Sidney Forstater, who was Leonard's chief financial officer at the time.

Tose's money troubles continued to snowball, though; he just couldn't stop spending or gambling. In the summer of 1977, the NFL threw him a much-needed life preserver. It persuaded the Ford family, which owned the Detroit Lions, to arrange a substantial loan for Leonard. The problem was, whenever Leonard had money, he quickly blew through it.

A few weeks after getting the loan, Leonard and Jim fired Forstater, who had tried to put a cap on the owner's free-spending ways. As the team's business manager, I had worked closely with him and became concerned about my own job security. I was concerned enough that I went to Leonard shortly after they got rid of Forstater and asked him whether I had anything to worry about. His exact words to me at the time were, "I have no problem with you, Leo. Go back to work."

But Jim apparently had other ideas. Six weeks later, the day after our first game that season, he called me into his office and fired me. I'd say I never saw it coming, but I did. Two days earlier, Kay and I happened to be at a dinner party hosted by a friend of ours, Mary Lou Duffy. She told Kay then that she had heard I was going to be fired. She even knew the names of the two people Jim was going to replace me with—Jim Borden and Hugh Ortman. Borden, a car dealer in South Jersey, was going to be the team's business manager. Ortman was going to take over as ticket manager. Not surprisingly, both were Villanova alums.

I went to the game the day after the dinner party and didn't say anything to anybody. Jim and Leonard acted like everything was hunky-dory. Then I went in Monday morning and Jim told me I was fired. That was one of the most devastating moments of my life. I mean, I had seven kids at home at the time, the oldest just 14. Kay and I were living paycheck to paycheck. What a terrible, desperate feeling.

I still remember the headline in the paper the next day: CARLIN FIRED BY EAGLES. This was 1977, and my son Leo had just started at St. Joe's Prep. He was on the freshman football team at the time. He has always been a very strong person, but when that story ran in the paper, he took some ribbing about it. He never told me about it, but I heard about it from others. That stuck with me for the rest of my life.

Getting rid of me wasn't a cost-cutting move. Like I said, they replaced me with two people who were paid twice what I had been making handling both jobs. After Jim fired me, I went to Leonard and asked him why I was being let go, what had changed during the six weeks since he told me I was safe. He wouldn't look at me, wouldn't answer my question. He just said, "Too late. I've made up my mind." To this day, I don't have a real answer for why I was let go.

The day after they fired me, Kay went in to get some things out of my office. She was fuming over what Jim and Leonard had done. Before she left the building, she went into the office where both Leonard and Jim were. She looked at both of them and told them, "I hope you rot in hell," and stormed out.

Gordon Forbes, the great sportswriter who covered the Eagles for the *Philadelphia Inquirer* back then, wrote at the time that firing me was Leonard's dumbest move since he tried to select draft picks.

That was more than 40 years ago, but the truth is, I've never gotten over it. I'll never forget the feeling of being hung out there to dry with seven kids. I did what I was told and got set up to be a fall guy. Every now and then, someone will mention those days, and it will all come rushing back to me. I still remember so vividly saying good-bye to everyone the day I was let go. One of those people was my good friend Eagles offensive tackle Stan Walters, who would become the team's radio analyst alongside Merrill Reese for 14 years after he retired in 1983. As I shook his hand in the locker room, I started crying like a baby. We just agreed to talk later. That scene was repeated as I spoke with other players, staff, and other associates.

I felt so betrayed by Jim; I thought we were friends. Ironically, Jim eventually was fired himself. In 1983 Leonard brought in his daughter, Susan Fletcher, to straighten out the financial mess he had made. When she saw what a disaster the place was, she fired Jim. A lot of people didn't like Susan or her methods. To my knowledge, she's the first and only person in NFL history ever to install a time clock in a team's executive offices. But the truth is, she was a really sharp businessperson. Not good enough to bail out her father, though; that would have taken a miracle worker. After a failed attempt to move the team to Phoenix in 1984, Leonard, with no other options, sold the team to Norman Braman.

One day about 20 years ago or so, I was in church and Jim came up to me. He was crying. He reached for my hand and said, "Leo, every day of my life since all of that happened, I've tried to think of a way to tell you how sorry I am for what I did to you." I looked at him and simply said, "We'll talk." We did eventually, in the back booth of a quiet restaurant on the Main Line. Just the two of us. I reminded him of many of the details of those days. Even years later, they still were fresh in my mind. He just kept apologizing and repeating that he had been wrong. He even offered to meet with my entire family and apologize to all of them.

I was bitter toward Jim for a long time. I mean, it was a very frightening time for my whole family and me. When it happened, I had no idea what I was going to do or how I was going to pay tuition for seven children. But there is nothing to be gained by holding a grudge, no matter how profound an effect the thing you're angry over had on your life. I've had a lot of time to reflect during the course of putting this book together. I realize that it took a lot of courage for Jim to come up to me years later and apologize for what happened. I'm grateful for that apology. I don't know if it matters to him anymore or not, but I've forgiven him.

Getting fired is not something I like to talk about. When people would ask me how long I had been with the Eagles, I would simply tell them I started there in 1960. I just didn't want to rehash what happened. Even today, it still hurts too much.

I opened a ticket office downtown in the John Wanamaker building, which helped pay the bills after the Eagles fired me. I also became the Stars' business manager for three years before returning to the Eagles as ticket manager in 1985, after Braman bought the team. When I returned, I was going to sell my ticket business, as I felt it might be a conflict of interest. But Norman encouraged me to keep it. He said we could use it as a downtown ticket office for the team.

When Leonard Tose found out I had been rehired by the Eagles, he actually called me and said, "Leo, you are back where you belong." Can you believe that? That just further confirmed for me that getting rid of me was never his idea in the first place.

When Leonard died in 2003, I actually went to his funeral. It was on Easter Sunday, but I still went. I remember his daughter Susan coming up to me and saying, "I know what this [day] is for you. Thank you for coming."

Chapter 13

My Olympic Moment

Not long after the Eagles let me go, I took a job in the 76ers' ticket office, but I didn't stay very long. Even with seven mouths to feed and Catholic school tuitions to pay, I just didn't like it there. When you come from the NFL, you're just used to a certain way of doing things. I had some job offers from other NFL teams, but with seven kids, moving wasn't really an option even if Kay and I wanted to. And we didn't. I'm a Philly guy, and she's a Philly girl.

Back in the day, the Globe Ticket Company used to sell the tickets for just about everything: circuses, plays, concerts, you name it. The International Olympic Committee had awarded Globe the ticket contract for the 1980 Winter Olympics in Lake Placid, New York. They initially tried to do it themselves, but the project was a little bit too much for the inexperienced people they had handling it.

This was the fall of 1979, about a year after I had been fired by the Eagles. The Winter Games were just a few months away, and Globe was really up against it. I was friendly with one of Globe's top executives, and he approached me about taking over the ticket distribution for the Winter Games.

The ticketing already was in serious trouble, and I was asked to help get them out of the jam. Even though I no longer was working for the Eagles, my friend Joel Ralph, who was the stadium operations manager at

I framed tickets from 16 of the events from the 1980 Winter Games. What an experience!

Veterans Stadium, let me use a big room in the basement of the Vet as a base of operations. I had 750,000 tickets down there and could only tell a few people what I was working on. I hired about 20 people to help me, and we worked day and night to get the job done.

The best part of it was that Globe was so grateful for helping them out, they brought Kay and me to Lake Placid for the Olympics. I'll never forget our plane landing on icy Lake Placid when we arrived there. We got to see the opening ceremony. We saw the great speed skater Eric Heiden and, of course, the U.S. hockey team, which upset Russia and won the gold medal that year in what would become forever known as the Miracle on Ice. What a great thrill that was. It was one of the great experiences of my life. I still have memorabilia on our walls at home from those Olympics.

Small-world department: Mike Eruzione, who was the captain of the gold medal–winning hockey team, had a younger brother, Vinny, who later was my son Leo's teammate on the Holy Cross football team.

Chapter 14

Kings of the Spring

I spent more than a half-century with the Eagles and loved every single minute of it. (Well, OK, not every single minute.) That said, one of the most exciting experiences of my career was working three-plus years for the Philadelphia Stars of the United States Football League.

The USFL was a pro football league that played in the spring. The season would start in February and run to mid-July. The USFL only lasted three years, from 1983 to 1985, but it's a time I'll never forget and will always relish.

The Stars were the league's best franchise, both on the field and off. We won two of the league's three championships and appeared in all three title games. More than a dozen of our players ended up playing in the NFL after the USFL folded. One of them, linebacker Sam Mills—who died of cancer in 2005—was one of 15 finalists for the Pro Football Hall of Fame in 2020.

The Stars were owned by three successful Philadelphia-area shopping mall developers: Myles Tanenbaum, Harold Schaeffer, and Art Powell. Their company, Kravco, built a number of malls across the country, including the King of Prussia mall. Tanenbaum, who was a successful tax attorney and a partner in the Philadelphia law firm of Wolf, Block, Schorr & Solis-Cohen, was the point man on the trio's USFL venture and became the team's managing general partner.

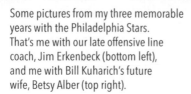

Some pictures from my three memorable years with the Philadelphia Stars. That's me with our late offensive line coach, Jim Erkenbeck (bottom left), and me with Bill Kuharich's future wife, Betsy Alber (top right).

Myles's first hire was Carl Peterson, who had been Dick Vermeil's player personnel chief with the Eagles. He became the Stars' president and general manager. I knew Carl from the Eagles, and he brought me on board as the team's business and ticket manager.

Carl and I ran into each other down in Sea Isle in the summer of 1982 and he told me about the spring league and the Stars. He asked me if I'd be interested in working in the Stars' front office, and we agreed to talk again when we both got back to the city. He said, "Do you want to do it?" I said, "Yes, I absolutely want to do it." I'm eternally grateful to Carl. He got me back into the game I love.

We pretty much started from square one. We had nothing, not even a pencil or notepad. The work was overwhelming at times; I never worked as hard in my life as I did in those three years with the Stars. But I wouldn't have traded it for the world. It was gratifying, and I met people who are dear friends to this day.

Early on, we worked out of the Kravco offices in King of Prussia. Eventually we leased space and built offices in Veterans Stadium, where we played our games for the first two seasons of the league's existence.

Every morning, I would get to my Kravco office by 7:00 AM or earlier. It had a big window that faced the parking lot. Each morning, Myles would knock on that window when he arrived and mouth the words, "Let's have coffee." I'd meet him in his office, and we'd end up drinking countless cups of coffee during those long sessions. There were times when I didn't get back to my own office until 3:00, and then I would have to start working on my own stuff.

As the team's business manager, most of the business aspects were left to me. And when you're starting from scratch, well, there's a lot to do—from ordering supplies to negotiating the team's radio contract to a hundred other things. I had to handle all of the franchise business, including insurance matters, policy meetings, and business plans, and a never-ending ticket campaign.

With former Stars head coach Jim Mora.

I helped negotiate our lease with the city to use Veterans Stadium. Myles and I met with the mayor at the time, Wilson Goode, and my good friend Joel Ralph, who was the stadium manager at the Vet. Since the USFL played in the spring, we weren't going head-to-head with the Eagles, but that didn't matter to Leonard Tose. He considered us a threat from the outset and was not at all happy to have us around.

Before we negotiated the Vet lease, Leonard ran into Myles and Carl one night at Bookbinder's, a popular bar and restaurant in the Society Hill section of Philadelphia. As was often the case with Leonard, he'd had a few too many, and he approached the table where Myles and Carl were seated. Leonard had been trying hard to prevent us from using the Vet for our games. That night at Bookbinder's, he offered to bet Myles a million dollars that his team would never get a lease with the city to play at the Vet. Myles should've taken the bet.

I was constantly chasing money with the Stars. We had a much better financial strategy than most USFL teams, but there were still constant cash-flow problems. I can remember often waiting frantically for our television payments from ABC and ESPN to be disbursed. But unlike a lot of teams in the league, we always paid our bills, even if we frequently had to call on the investors for another chunk of their dough.

Myles could be a tough guy to work for. He was very excitable, and when he got pissed, he could be a real asshole. Myles was an accountant and a lawyer, a background that gave him an advantage in dealing with his adversaries but that often made it excruciating for the people who worked for him.

Myles used to hold marathon meetings early on when we were getting started. I remember one that lasted 24 hours. I kid you not. We took breaks to eat and sleep, but when we woke up, we went right back into the meeting room. Myles dominated the whole meeting. We weren't allowed to call anybody or do anything. I couldn't even call Kay. I think we were allowed to take bathroom breaks, but I can't swear to it.

I remember another meeting we had, this one after we had moved into our offices at the Vet. Myles was the consummate attorney. He would prepare his case and his questions before he even got into the room. At one point in the meeting, Myles turned to me and asked how many season tickets we had sold; I said 15,000. Then he turned to a marketing person we had early on named Thelma and asked the same question. Thelma was very persnickety, very Main Line–ish. In a somewhat dismissive tone, she said, "Well, Myles, we haven't checked." Myles looked at her in disbelief and said, "You're handling the budget for my marketing department and you don't know how many season tickets we've sold? Maybe you shouldn't be our marketing director." He proceeded to rip her apart in front of everybody; it was horrible. I didn't see Thelma much after that.

Shortly after joining the Stars, Carl hired Bob Moore to be the team's temporary public relations director. Bob had been the sports information director at Drexel University. One of my first assignments from Carl was to interview Bob and see if we should hire him on a full-time basis. It ended up being a no-brainer. Bob was bright, clever, sincere, funny, talented, caring, and just plain fun. He's still one of my very best friends in life.

A couple years after the USFL went under, Carl became the president and general manager of the NFL's Kansas City Chiefs. He hired Bob as the Chiefs' PR director. Bob was with the Chiefs for nearly 25 years before finally retiring a few years ago. He spent his last few years with the Chiefs as the team historian, and spearheaded the construction of the Chiefs' Hall of Honor.

I'll never forget an early incident involving Bob and Myles. Sports apparel companies frequently gave out clothing to teams. One day, Bob made the mistake of wearing a jacket with the Stars logo that he had received from one of those apparel companies. Myles saw it and immediately said, "Man, I really like that jacket." Bob told him the company had sent one to each team's PR guy and general manager. All of a sudden, Myles, who always put his hands in your face when he was talking to you, said, "You don't get the jacket. I get the jacket." I mean, you would've thought Bob had just stolen Myles's Gucci loafers. Bob took that jacket off so fast it almost caused a tornado in the room. He handed it to Myles and never saw it again. Well, except on Myles.

I'll never forget another episode with Myles, this one in 1983. We were in our first season. The Philadelphia 76ers had won the NBA championship and the city was throwing a victory parade for them. Carl and I were down at the Vet that morning. Myles called and wanted to have a meeting up at Kravco. Carl told Myles the parade was coming down Broad Street and we weren't going to be able to make it up there and hung up the phone. Well, Myles called me back and insisted I get up there, come hell or a parade with two million spectators.

Needless to say, traffic was a mess. The Blue Route hadn't been built yet. At one point, I pulled over and called Myles to tell him I didn't think I was going to be able to get up there. He promptly said, "I don't care about the fucking parade. Get your ass up here."

Well, I finally made it up there about two hours late. We met in a restaurant called Charlie's Place. He proceeded to read me the riot act. Then, after he got done blasting me in front of everybody in the place, he stood up and put his arms around me and hugged me. That was the meeting. The changing moods with Myles were brutal; he was a very volatile guy.

Despite Myles's mercurial temperament, he was a good businessman who put together a top-flight organization. It started with Carl, who had helped Dick Vermeil put together a Super Bowl team with the Eagles and did an incredible job of building the Stars and turning them into the league's best team in its brief existence.

Carl and Myles's first head coaching hire was George Perles, who was the Pittsburgh Steelers' defensive coordinator at the time. But Perles never ended up coaching a game for us. Shortly after he took the job, his alma mater, Michigan State, offered him the head coaching job there, and George took it.

George wasn't around long, but I liked him. He was a funny guy. We were still working out of the Kravco offices at the time. We'd have players who we had signed hanging out up there, and Kravco's secretarial pool of young ladies would go nuts. They all wanted to work for us. Perles would tell them to see me in the morning and I'd give them a job with us. I knew nothing about it, of course. But there they were the next day, outside my office, telling me George had told them to see me about a job. I'd have to tell them George was only kidding. Some of the Kravco secretaries did end up being hired by the Stars, though, including Betsy Alber, who became Carl's executive secretary. Betsy met her future husband during the three-plus years she worked for the Stars—our player personnel director, Bill Kuharich, who was the youngest of Joe's two sons. Bill was one of many Stars coaches and front-office executives who went on to work in the NFL.

After Perles left for Michigan State, Myles made a run at Penn State's coach, Joe Paterno. He even threw a shore house in Sea Isle City into his offer to Paterno. JoePa actually was tempted but ended up saying thanks but no thanks.

With our first training camp just two weeks away, Carl ended up hiring Jim Mora, who was the defensive coordinator for the New England Patriots at the time. Jim ended up being an absolutely wonderful choice. After the USFL died, Jim was an NFL head coach for 15 years, 11 with the New Orleans Saints and 4 with the Indianapolis Colts. He won 125 games, which is the 31st most in NFL history. He had five straight winning seasons with a Saints franchise that hadn't had one winning season in its previous 19 years of existence. Carl and Jim built the Stars into the league's very best franchise. Jim's teams won 41 of 54 regular-season games in three seasons. We appeared in all three league championship games, losing the first one and winning the next two.

Having been the Eagles' personnel boss, Carl knew where all the bodies were buried. He brought in NFL castoffs such as offensive lineman Chuck Commiskey, safety Mike Lush, quarterback Chuck Fusina, linebackers Sam Mills and Glenn Howard, tight ends Steve Folsom and Ken Dunek, and wide receivers Scott Fitzkee and Tom Donovan. He lured NFL veterans such as defensive tackle Pete Kugler and linebacker John Bunting to the Stars. In addition, his good friend Lynn Stiles, who succeeded him as the Eagles' player personnel boss, would give him a sneak peek at the list of players NFL teams were about to release so he could have first crack at signing them.

Carl also drafted and signed top young college players such as offensive linemen Irv Eatman and Bart Oates, running back Kelvin Bryant, defensive end William Fuller, linebackers Mike Johnson and George Jamison, cornerback/safety Antonio Gibson, and punter Sean Landeta. Eighteen Stars players went on to play 30 or more games or make 15 or more starts in the NFL after the USFL folded. Five former Stars players made a total of 18 Pro Bowl appearances.

Carl was one of four Stars front-office people who went on to become NFL general managers. The other three were Bill Kuharich (Saints), assistant player personnel director Rod Graves (Cardinals), and Bill's administrative assistant, Terry Bradway (Jets).

Catching up with Jim Mora and his wife, Connie, at the Stars' 30-year reunion.

Numerous others in the Stars organization went on to have NFL careers. As mentioned, Jim Mora was a longtime NFL head coach, but there were three Stars coaches who later became NFL head coaches. Jim's defensive coordinator, Vince Tobin, spent five seasons as the Arizona Cardinals' head coach and his defensive backs coach, Dom Capers, was the head coach of the Carolina Panthers and Houston Texans. Several of Mora's assistants went on to long and successful careers as NFL assistants. Carl Smith, who was Jim's quarterbacks coach with the Stars and later his offensive coordinator in New Orleans, is an offensive consultant for the Houston Texans.

The city of Philadelphia embraced the Stars. The Eagles, after making it to the Super Bowl in 1980, quickly got old and fell into a state of disrepair, which helped our popularity. They finished 3–6 in 1982's strike-shortened season, then went 5–11 in 1983 and 6–9–1 in 1984.

If the Stars had played the Eagles during that time, the Stars probably would have beaten them. By our second year, we had a season-ticket base of 25,000 and were regularly drawing crowds of 35,000 to 40,000, which was pretty damn good.

After we won the league championship in 1984, the city threw us a victory parade. More than 50,000 lined the eight-block parade route. Another 30,000 jammed JFK Plaza for the post-parade celebration. It wasn't anywhere close to the magnitude of the Eagles' parade after they won Super Bowl LII, but it was pretty impressive for a two-year-old football team that played in the spring. And it spoke volumes about the passion of the city's sports fans.

Six days after we won the championship in '84, we flew to Europe for an exhibition game against another USFL team, the Tampa Bay Bandits. The game was kind of hastily thrown together, and when we got there, we realized we hadn't brought any per-diem money for the players. Carl told me to go to a bank and take care of it. Well, this was 1984, in a foreign country. Getting funds quickly was easier said than done. Bob Moore and I went to a nearby bank. I said, "Listen, my name is Leo Carlin. I work for the football team that's going to be playing at Wembley Stadium this weekend and need whatever thousand dollars." The teller looked curiously at me and said, "You won't get that in all of London, Yank." I tried to make it clear to him that I wasn't there alone and pointed at Bob, our esteemed public relations director, who was asleep against the wall, obviously suffering from jet lag. He looked like a derelict. I can't remember how we did it, but we finally got the money for our players.

The Brits weren't all that friendly to us on that trip. They may be crazy about American football now, but back then, not so much. Especially a spring league most of them had never heard of. I remember this guy selling papers in front of the hotel. Every time he saw me, he said, "Go away, Yank. We don't want you here." On the last day, as our bus was getting ready to pull away from the hotel to take us to the airport for the trip home, the guy got on the bus and said, "Go home, Yanks, and don't ever come back. But if you do, don't bring any of that chocolate you gave to my mother during the war. She still has the shits from it."

Chapter 15
The Donald

The USFL was very popular in the spring and could've carved out a nice little niche during that time of the year. But a few owners, most notably Donald Trump—who bought the New Jersey Generals after the USFL's first year—weren't really interested in a spring league.

Trump bought into the league with the idea of moving to the fall and going head-to-head with the NFL so he could force a merger with the NFL. But that never happened. The USFL filed an antitrust suit against the NFL in 1984. The USFL actually won the suit, but with the arrogant, unlikeable Trump insisting on being the face of the league during the trial, the jury awarded us all of three dollars in treble damages. That jury award essentially was the death knell for the USFL.

Trump's level of culpability in the demise of the USFL depends on who you talk to. If you talk to Trump, he'll tell you that not only did he not kill the USFL, he almost singlehandedly kept it afloat during the final two years of its short existence. Others believe the league might've lived a long and reasonably healthy life if Trump hadn't convinced the other owners to move to the fall.

The truth, as it often does, lies somewhere in the middle. The league was having problems even before Trump bought in after the first season. In their haste to be competitive and taken seriously, many of the 12 original owners ignored the league's original five-year plan, which called for judicious spending on players early on. "The idea was, let's crawl before we walk and walk before we run," Carl Peterson said. "The first year you'd have one large signing guy. The second year, two. The third, three. You'd pay those guys whatever you thought you could afford. But teams immediately violated that."

The Michigan Panthers, who beat the Stars in the first USFL Championship Game, signed three players off the Pittsburgh Steelers' offensive line. Other teams quickly followed suit. While the league was doing an impressive job of acquiring talent, whether top college players or NFL veterans, it wasn't generating nearly enough revenue from television and ticket sales to cover the cost of paying them. Even with TV deals with ABC and ESPN, the league lost more than $30 million in its first year. Some of the league's owners were equipped to deal with those kinds of financial losses, but most weren't. The league had to give the Chicago franchise $30,000 in cash before their opening game of the second season just so they could pay for their uniforms. We had payrolls that quickly reached the level of the smaller payrolls in the NFL. But NFL teams were making $14 million a year in TV revenue back then; USFL teams were making $1 million.

The league expanded from 12 to 18 teams in its second season mainly because many of the existing teams needed the expansion fees to stay afloat. But while the expansion money helped teams out in the short term, it was just a bad idea. The last thing a struggling young league needs is too many teams. The league ended up cutting back to 14 teams for its third and final season in 1985, but even that was too many.

Trump came aboard after the first season, buying the New Jersey Generals from Oklahoma oilman J. Walter Duncan for $8.5 million. His presence immediately raised the league's profile in the country's largest media market. He put the Generals on the back page of the city's tabloids. When he spoke, the media listened and wrote about it. Trump made an offer to the Giants' future Hall of Fame linebacker Lawrence Taylor. He signed the Cleveland Browns' Pro Bowl quarterback Brian Sipe. He made a very public pitch for Miami Dolphins coach Don Shula.

Trump was the ultimate salesman. Even though Shula had no intention of jumping leagues, CBS's *The NFL Today*, the top-rated NFL pregame program, brought Trump on for an interview, which absolutely infuriated the NFL. Trump went on the program and said they'd had "great negotiations" with Shula and that they had agreed on all of the "business points" of a contract. He said the one sticking point, and one he wouldn't agree to, was Shula's demand for a unit in Trump Tower. Then he spent the next five minutes turning *The NFL Today* into an infomercial for Trump Tower. I don't like the guy, but it was ingenious.

Trump made it clear from the minute he bought into the league that he felt it had no future in the spring. He called the spring a "wasteland" for football. "If God had wanted football in the spring, he wouldn't have invented baseball," he would tell people. He called for a vote on a move to the fall at the very first league meeting he attended after buying the Generals. "Even if we had cut our losses in the spring, there was no foreseeable chance of making a profit," Trump wrote in his 1987 book *Trump: The Art of the Deal*. "And a lot of our weaker owners couldn't afford to lose another dime. We needed to take radical action. And that's what I stood up and said."

Trump saw the USFL as a way of getting what he really wanted, which was an NFL team. He felt that if the league moved to the fall, it could force a merger with the NFL, either by getting a fall TV contract, or, more likely, filing an antitrust suit against the NFL. Basically, the USFL was Trump's attempt to get into a club—the NFL—that wasn't offering him admittance. "He's never been a team player," Bob Rose, who was the USFL's director of public relations, said. "Like everything else he's been involved in, Donald was in it for Donald. He clearly didn't give a shit what the other owners thought."

Three months after he bought the Generals, one of Trump's assistants, Jay Seltzer, sent a memo to Myles Tanenbaum, a staunch spring advocate, about the potential outcome of a merger with the NFL if they moved to the fall. He said some teams almost certainly would be left out, but "presumably they would be 'paid off' by reimbursement plus a profit of some proportions." Tanenbaum wrote back to Seltzer that Trump's merger strategy "troubles me greatly."

Tanenbaum, who passed away in 2012 at the age of 82, strongly believed in the concept of pro football in the spring. The Stars became the USFL's showcase team by spending judiciously on a few star players, drafting smartly, and signing NFL castoffs who made the most of a second chance. But many of the league's other owners panicked as their financial losses mounted in the spring. The more Trump talked about big money in the fall, the better it sounded. In August 1984, just a month after the USFL's second season ended, the owners voted 12–2 to move to the fall beginning in 1986. Tanenbaum was one of the two dissenting votes.

But after the league suspended operations in the late summer of 1986, even Tanenbaum reluctantly admitted Trump's move-to-the-fall strategy probably had been the USFL's only survival option. "I will defend Donald in this regard," he told the *Philadelphia Inquirer*'s Chuck Newman in August 1986. "We could not generate enough revenue to continue to operate [in the spring] because people don't watch football on TV in the spring."

Trump ultimately found an important ally in his move-to-the-fall campaign in Chicago White Sox minority owner Eddie Einhorn. He was almost as influential as Trump in convincing the other owners to move to the fall. Einhorn, a former TV executive who had helped negotiate many of Major League Baseball's TV deals, was supposed to take over the league's financially troubled Chicago franchise and spearhead the USFL's negotiations for a new TV deal if it moved to the fall.

Einhorn carried a lot of weight because of his affiliation with the White Sox and his experience on baseball's broadcast committee. He told the owners one of two things would happen if they moved to the fall. Either a number of teams would be absorbed into the NFL as expansion teams or we were going to win the lawsuit, because there was no doubt in his mind that, even back then, the NFL monopolized programming for pro football in the fall.

He was right on the second part. Trouble is, everybody that voted for moving to the fall thought there would be a big revenue windfall, either from a TV deal in the fall or damages from our lawsuit. It didn't happen. Einhorn never tried very hard to negotiate a fall TV deal with any of the major networks. Fox wasn't a sports broadcasting player yet, and ABC, NBC, and CBS all were televising NFL games in the fall, which clearly supported the USFL's claim that the NFL was a monopoly.

Less than a week after the three-dollar antitrust verdict in July 1986, the USFL's owners voted to suspend the 1986 season and the league never played another game. Trump has readily admitted that he was the main reason for the chump-change damage award. In one of the most curious decisions of the 42-day trial, he was the only USFL owner the league's attorney, Harvey Myerson, put on the stand. Let's just say he did not come off as sympathetic. "I was part of the problem," Trump admitted in his book. "As a witness, I was well-spoken and professional, I think. But that probably played into the NFL's hands. From day one, they painted me as a vicious, greedy, Machiavellian billionaire, intent only on serving my selfish ends at everyone's expense." It didn't take a lot of paint. Trump might be the only guy in the world who could make the NFL's owners look like the Mormon Tabernacle Choir.

Steve Ehrhart, the league's first executive director and later the president of the USFL's Memphis Showboats, said he learned later that the NFL conducted a mock trial before the actual trial. In the mock trial, the USFL won a huge verdict. That caused the NFL to change their whole strategy. Instead of trying to defend their individual predatory actions, such as the infamous Harvard Business School study about how to kill the USFL, they went after Donald Trump. They made Donald the face of the league. It was a very smart move. They portrayed him as the rich, brash guy trying to kill the poor, little NFL. And Myerson and the rest of the USFL's lawyers played right into that by putting Donald on the stand. The USFL people asked Myerson why he didn't put other owners on the stand, such as the guy in Birmingham, Marvin Warner, who was trying to do some good things for his community. But Myerson was playing to Trump. He was a New York–suspenders kind of guy.

Before the verdict, the NFL was concerned enough about a possible negative trial outcome to discuss a possible merger with the USFL. The NFL talked to the USFL people about taking in a couple teams. But Myerson and Trump and the rest of the USFL negotiators wanted at least four teams, or even six. There was no way the NFL ever was going to agree to that.

Ehrhart thinks the USFL still might have had a chance to survive if it had gone ahead and played in the fall of 1986. The league was down to eight teams. Just two of them, Trump's Generals and the Tampa Bay Bandits, were in NFL markets. They still had a TV deal with ESPN. But the embarrassing three-dollar verdict had broken most of the owners' will to go on. Plus, Myerson had advised them that not playing in '86 was a wiser legal strategy. He gave a speech about how this was the most unique and unusual verdict in history and that the NFL had violated the law. He said if we just held off playing, we'd win on appeal and get an injunction against them preventing them from being on all three television networks. In March 1988 a federal appeals court upheld the '86 verdict and damage award. The USFL never got an injunction against the NFL. Myerson, whose nickname was Heavy Hitter Harvey, spent five years in prison in the 1990s for tax fraud and overbilling clients. He died in 2012.

I'll never forget when we played Trump's team in the 1984 USFL playoffs. We couldn't play the game at Veterans Stadium because the Phillies were using the stadium, so we had to move it to Franklin Field. Trump, who actually went to Penn, was furious. He felt the game should've been moved to Giants Stadium in the Meadowlands, where his team, the Generals, played, even though we had finished with a better record than the Generals. Trump kept saying Franklin Field was "a dump" and a "bush league place to play." He looked around Franklin Field before the game and said, "This is terrible. Tell Myles we should've taken this game to the Meadowlands." I said, "Well, if your team had managed to win more games than us, we would be playing it up there." He just turned his back to me and walked away.

The Stars actually ended up playing the 1985 season in Baltimore because of the potential move to the fall, though we continued to practice that season in Philadelphia at the University of Pennsylvania. Despite those challenging circumstances, we still managed to win a second straight league championship. The team was invited to the White House after the victory. I stayed back to handle some team and personal business, including an interview for my old job with the Eagles.

Tose, who had bought the Eagles from Jerry Wolman in 1969 for $16.1 million, sold it in March 1985 to West Philly native and Miami car dealer Norman Braman for $65 million. Jim Murray was long gone. Harry Gamble, who had become the team's general manager, and Mimi Box, who was the team's chief financial officer, approached me about coming back. Mimi, who spent 16 years in the Eagles' front office from 1983 to 1999, was instrumental in bringing me back to the organization, and I can't thank her enough. She's been a longtime friend.

Before I left, I had been both the ticket manager and the business manager. I made it clear when I talked to them that I was only interested in coming back as the ticket manager. They were fine with that. I threw myself back into my work with them. After being away for nearly eight years, I was back home.

In June 2017, more than 30 years after the USFL had shuttered, the team held a reunion at Chickie's & Pete's, the popular South Philly bar and restaurant. It was unbelievable how many former Stars players, coaches, executives, and members of the support staff turned out for that get-together. We shared a lot of memories that night and shed a lot of tears.

I will always consider myself an Eagle, but those three years with the Stars—when we built something special from nothing—will always hold a special place in my heart. What made that whole experience so special was that we all had the same cause. We all were in the same fight. It brought all of us closer together.

Chapter 16
The Man in France

There is little doubt in my mind that Jeffrey Lurie has been the best owner in the history of the Philadelphia Eagles, or at least during the half-century I worked for the organization.

Some people might be surprised by the guy I feel is second to Lurie: Norman Braman. That's right, Norman Braman. My measuring stick here isn't wins and losses or playoff appearances, though the Eagles did manage to have five double-digit-win seasons and made the playoffs four times in the nine years Norman owned the team from 1985 until selling it to Lurie in the spring of 1994 for $185 million.

I know Braman wasn't liked by a lot of fans and players. OK, he was despised by them. Even though he grew up in West Philly, many Eagles fans considered him a South Florida carpetbagger who cared more about making money than winning games. Indeed, Norman was a businessman all the way. There were situations where other owners might have done things differently, where they would have let their heart overrule their head. But that wasn't Norman.

Fans often forget that an NFL franchise—or any professional sports team, for that matter—is, at its foundation, a business. Norman respected the fans and cared about winning, but he also was a businessman who preached fiscal responsibility—probably too much to suit his critics, which included most of the team's players.

But from my own narrow personal perspective as an Eagles front-office employee, he was a terrific guy to work for. Night-and-day better than Leonard, who is recalled much more fondly by Eagles fans than Norman, even though Leonard tried to take the Eagles away from them and move them to another city to help him deal with his debt problems. With Norman, if you were loyal to him, he was loyal to you.

I remember once I was having a really, really busy week. Actually, all weeks were busy under Norman's ownership. But he called me in and said, "Listen, I know you've been working really hard. Take this as a gesture of my appreciation for all you're doing." He pulled out some jewelry and cuff links and gave them to me. We're not talking cheap knockoffs; this was expensive stuff.

I remember a couple years after I came back to the Eagles, we had a home game on Labor Day weekend against an AFC team—I think it was the Cincinnati Bengals. That never was a good weekend for us attendance-wise because a lot of our fans would spend that holiday weekend down the shore. The holiday combined with an unattractive opponent resulted in 4,000 unsold tickets, which meant the game was blacked out in Philly.

But the weather turned out to be gorgeous, and we got a tremendous walk-up crowd—to the point that we ended up selling standing-room-only tickets. We had ticket computerization back then, but it wasn't nearly as sophisticated as it is today. Gate-sale situations like that one were a challenge to handle back then. But we got it done and everything turned out well.

Anyway, the game was over and I was driving home. I used to drive home after 1:00 games at about 7:00 or 7:30 in order to avoid traffic. I lived in Bryn Mawr at the time but would usually go up Broad Street rather than get on the Schuylkill near the stadium because it had the least amount of traffic.

Now, I'm not what you'd call an aggressive driver. I don't give the finger to other drivers or yell at them when they do something to me. It's a waste of time. It just shortens your life getting upset about stuff like that. So I was going around city hall that night and there was this guy nudging me out. I just ignored him and kept on going. But he did it again and then started blowing his horn. I looked over and, lo and behold, it was Norman. God almighty, it scared the hell out of me. He motioned to me to roll my window down. I rolled it down and he said, "Leo, I'm headed out of town. But I wanted to tell you that was a goddamn good job you did for all of us today. I want you to know how much I appreciate it." That was Norman, and that's something I never forgot. I assure you the owner before him never bothered to take the time to say something like that.

Norman used to host a pregame get-together in the Eagles' offices at the Vet, with a lot of VIPs in attendance. I always hated those things because I would have to walk through the party to get to my office. One time, as I was walking through, Norman came over to me, put his hand up, and asked everyone to be quiet. We're talking a couple hundred people at this thing. Anyway, he said, "Attention, everybody. I just want you to know that we are privileged to have this gentleman in our organization. This is Leo Carlin, who most of you know."

Norman would do things like that, not just with me but with others he liked and respected. I know a lot of people outside the organization at the time, and even some inside the organization, didn't have the same opinion of Norman that I did. But he always treated me well.

Every year he would take the entire organization to Miami for a long weekend after the season. It was a fantastic experience. We would sail up the Intracoastal Waterway and over to some islands on a party boat. What was impressive was that Norman knew everybody's names and their spouses' names too. Pretty impressive for a guy in his position. There are owners in the NFL who don't know the name of their personnel director.

I'm told the late Phillies president David Montgomery was the same way. He made a point of knowing the names of everyone in the organization, including interns, so if he walked into the lunchroom and

On the mic at an event during the Braman era.

they were sitting there, he'd be able to address them by name. Not many owners or executives care enough about their employees to do that.

Norman would have me serve as the emcee on the party boat. I enjoyed doing it even though I always was a little nervous. The trips were a good bonding experience for the whole organization.

Norman's wife, Irma, was a lovely, lovely person. She was down-to-earth, and like Norman, you could have a nice conversation with her. One day, I came out of my office and happened to share an elevator with the Bramans. On the ride down, Irma was saying that she needed to get to Center City but didn't have a car with her. I couldn't help but notice she was wearing a shitload of expensive jewelry. Norman, who grew up in West Philly, turned to her and said, "Why don't you go down to the corner [of Broad and Pattison] and take the subway? Hop on it, and you'll be there in no time." Well, she turned to him and gave him a death stare. She was pissed not only that he suggested that but that he said it in front of me. I was choking trying not to laugh. She got to Center City somehow that day, though I'm fairly certain it wasn't on the subway. Just the fact that he had the guts to say that to her, though, was rather amusing.

Norman's biggest regret as the Eagles' owner clearly was hiring Buddy Ryan. He bought the team from Tose in the spring of 1985. Marion Campbell had succeeded Dick Vermeil as the head coach in 1983 after Dick burned out and abruptly quit following the strike-shortened 1982 season. Marion, whose nickname was the Swamp Fox, had played on the Eagles' 1960 championship team. He was one of the nicest men in the world and had done an outstanding job as Vermeil's defensive coordinator. But Dick didn't leave Swampy a very good team. Marion inherited an aging club that went 5–11 in 1983 and 6–9–1 in 1984. To make matters worse, Dick's personnel chief, Carl Peterson, also left after the '82 season for the USFL. His replacement, Lynn Stiles, was a nice man and had been an excellent special teams coach earlier in his career. But evaluating talent was his strong point.

In 1985 the Eagles lost four of their first five games, including twice to the New York Giants, then rebounded to win five of their next six. But then they faded down the stretch, losing four in a row. Braman fired Campbell after a West Coast loss to the San Diego Chargers in the next-to-last game of the season and made defensive backs coach Fred Bruney the team's interim head coach.

Poor Fred, who was one of the nicest people you'd ever want to meet, thought he had a chance to permanently replace Campbell if his team played well in their final game against the Minnesota Vikings. The Eagles ended up beating the Vikings that day, 37–35. The 37 points were the most the Eagles had scored in a game in four years. In his postgame news conference with reporters, Fred said he was hopeful the team's impressive performance would help his chances of replacing Campbell. But Fred never was a serious candidate. The Eagles could have beaten the Vikings 100–0 that day and there still was no way in hell Norman was going to make him the next head coach.

Norman was looking for a bigger name as his first head coaching hire. Or at least the relative of a bigger name. Even before the Eagles took the field against the Vikings, he had zeroed in on David Shula, the son of then Miami Dolphins' coach, Don Shula. David had been a wide receiver at Dartmouth, spent one season with the Baltimore Colts as a wide receiver and punt returner, then went into the family business, serving as the wide receivers coach on his father's staff in Miami.

Never mind that David was just 25 years old. Norman lived in Miami Beach and knew and liked Don, and he figured the apple doesn't fall far from the tree. He thought hiring David would be an ingenious idea. Until David asked for a 10-year contract. Norman didn't like being used in contract negotiations or business deals. As soon as David Shula's agent mentioned the 10-year contract, Norman crossed him off his list.

As for Bruney, he spent more than 30 years as an NFL assistant coach with five teams. He was considered one of the league's top defensive backs coaches but retired without ever getting a head coaching opportunity beyond that one game with the Eagles in 1985. Fred retired from coaching in 1997 and passed away in 2016 at the age of 84.

Norman's second choice was my good friend Jim Mora, who had won two USFL championships with the Philadelphia Stars. Jim would have made a terrific Eagles coach. He was extremely popular in Philly because of his success with the Stars. He had that Vermeil-like charisma. Norman offered him the job, but Jim was wary of working for him.

When Norman made an issue of including the money from the coach's weekly radio show as part of his salary, Jim felt Norman was more concerned with pinching pennies than getting the best coach. He walked away from the Eagles job and accepted a head coaching offer from New Orleans Saints general manager Jim Finks. Jim spent 11 years with the Saints and 4 more with the Indianapolis Colts. The Saints hadn't made the playoffs in their 19-year existence before Jim arrived in the Big Easy. He got them to the postseason in his second year there. Jim ended up winning 125 games as an NFL head coach. That's the 31st most in league history.

On the rebound after being rejected by Mora, Norman quickly zeroed in on the Chicago Bears' popular defensive coordinator, Buddy Ryan, who was coming off an impressive Super Bowl victory, after which his defensive players had carried him off the field. Norman didn't talk to a lot of people about Ryan but had read a glowing story on him in the *New York Times* and thought Buddy would be a perfect plan C. I'll talk a lot more about Buddy Ryan in the next chapter, but it's important to include him here for context.

It didn't take long for Norman to regret hiring Ryan. I know many of the players who played for Buddy loved him and would've killed for him. Same with many Eagles fans, who loved Buddy's fuck-you attitude. But truth be known, he wasn't a very nice guy.

In Ryan's second season as head coach, the NFL players staged a 24-day strike. The NFL countered by bringing in replacement players to play games for three weeks. Ryan, a former army sergeant, loathed coaching the replacement players and made no secret of it, which helped him bond with the regular players when they eventually came back but infuriated the hell out of Braman.

The Eagles lost all three of their replacement games and finished 7–8 that year. After the Eagles' final game, Ryan infuriated Braman even more when he held a mock awards ceremony at his season wrap-up news conference and presented "scab rings" to player personnel director Joe Woolley and George Azar, who was the assistant to club president Harry Gamble. Woolley and Azar had been tasked with signing replacement players for the Eagles during the strike. "We went to a lot of expense; the coaching staff, equipment people, and trainers all got together and put in money and bought George and Joe a couple of scab rings for all they did for us to get that scab personnel," Ryan said sarcastically.

From that point on, Braman and Ryan didn't even try to hide their contempt for each other. Ryan would refer to Braman as "the man in France," a reference to Norman's villa in the South of France, where he often vacationed during the summer while the Eagles were conducting training camp.

Braman's poor relationship with Ryan and the team's players, as well as the fans, made life extremely difficult for Gamble, who played the good cop to Norman's bad cop. Harry had been the head coach at the University of Pennsylvania for 10 years but was fired after the 1980 season. Dick Vermeil gave him a job with the Eagles as a volunteer assistant coach in 1981. Four years later, just before he sold the Eagles to Braman, Leonard Tose shocked everyone, including Harry, by making him the team's general manager.

After Braman bought the team, the assumption was that he would let Harry go and replace him with someone with more NFL front-office experience. But he took a quick liking to Harry. Instead of firing Harry, he added president to his job description. Harry was a very likeable guy. He ruled with a gentleness you don't often see but could be firm when he had to. Aside from Buddy, he had the complete respect of all of the Eagles employees.

As I mentioned earlier, Norman preached fiscal responsibility. Every contract negotiation with a player was a war. There were 14 training camp holdouts in Norman's first year as the team's owner, including his starting quarterback, Ron Jaworski, and his star wide receiver, Mike Quick. Since Norman typically went to France in early July and didn't return until right before the start of the season, it was left to Gamble to try to make peace with players and get everybody into camp. His favorite phrase every time a reporter asked him about the status of a holdout was, "We're keeping the lines of communication open."

I remember how cautiously Harry proceeded in 1985 before the Eagles signed Hall of Fame defensive end Reggie White. Reggie had played in the USFL with the Memphis Showboats. The Eagles had acquired his NFL rights in 1984 in a supplemental draft of USFL players.

By the summer of 1985, the USFL was, for all intents and purposes, dead. It had voted a year earlier to move to the fall in 1986, but after the three-dollar judgment discussed earlier, it had become pretty clear that wasn't going to happen. Teams were disbanding and letting star players such as White negotiate buyouts with the NFL teams that held their rights. White's agent, Patrick Forte, approached Gamble that summer about Reggie signing with the Eagles. White was one of the best players in the USFL. He would become one of the NFL's best-ever defensive players and a first-ballot Hall of Famer.

But while other NFL teams were signing USFL players, Gamble was fearful of getting sued by White's USFL team, the Showboats, and negotiations moved at a snail's pace. At one point a frustrated Forte, who, ironically enough, would later join the Eagles' front office, accused Harry of lacking the *cojones* to get a deal done. "A classic case of no balls," was what a frustrated Forte told reporters. It wasn't until the third week of the 1985 regular season that Gamble finally pulled the trigger on a deal with

Reggie. They bought out the remaining three years of his contract with the Showboats. Harry and the Eagles never got sued.

Reggie ended up being worth every penny of that buyout. In his first game with the Eagles, he registered 10 tackles and had 2.5 sacks. Reggie played eight seasons for the Eagles and had 124 sacks in 121 games with the team. He ended up becoming the name plaintiff in the players' lawsuit against the league that spawned free agency, and he signed a four-year, $17 million deal with the Green Bay Packers in 1993. That was huge, huge money back then. Now it's what a journeyman cornerback gets in free agency. Reggie spent six years with the Packers and helped them win a Super Bowl.

Like many Eagles players, Reggie disliked Norman with a passion. He was openly critical of the Eagles owner and believed, like many of the fans, that Norman cared more about making money than winning a Super Bowl. When Reggie became a free agent in 1993, it was reported that Norman didn't even make Reggie an offer. Norman has disputed that. What was indisputable was that Reggie had no interest in playing for a team that was owned by Norman Braman. He could have offered him a billion dollars and I doubt Reggie would have stayed in Philadelphia. He hated the Eagles owner that much. A year later Braman sold the Eagles to Jeffrey Lurie. White said later that if Lurie had owned the team in 1993, he never would have left.

White was every bit as dominant in Green Bay as he was in Philadelphia. He helped lead the Packers to a Super Bowl title in 1996. In 1998, at the age of 36, he had 16 quarterback sacks. He retired after the '98 season. He signed with the Carolina Panthers in 2000 but retired for good after that season. Then, like his good friend and teammate Jerome Brown, Reggie died too young. On the day after Christmas in 2004, Reggie passed away in his sleep at the age of 43. The cause of death was cardiac arrhythmia, which was triggered by complications related to sleep apnea.

A year later, in his first year of eligibility, Reggie White was a unanimous selection for the Hall of Fame. His wife, Sara, said Reggie had said before his death that he wanted to go into the Hall as both a Packer and an Eagle.

Buddy Ryan coached the Eagles for five seasons. As much as I disliked the guy, he was a defensive genius and put together one of the league's best defenses, led by White, Jerome Brown, Clyde Simmons, Byron Evans, Eric Allen, and Seth Joyner. The problem was, Buddy didn't have a clue how to build an offense. He thought he could just convert defensive linemen into serviceable offensive linemen. His idea of an offensive game plan was to tell quarterback Randall Cunningham to run around and make a play with his legs.

After finishing 5–10–1 and 7–8 in Ryan's first two seasons as head coach, the Eagles won the NFC East in 1988 with a 10–6 record. They had double-digit wins and made the playoffs in 1989 and '90 as well. But much to the chagrin of Braman and Eagles fans, Ryan's teams never were able to win a game in the postseason. In the Eagles' three one-and-done

Out to dinner with former Eagles owner Norman Braman (far left).

playoff losses in 1988, '89, and '90, Cunningham completed just 53.6 percent of his passes and failed to throw a single touchdown pass. The Eagles scored a total of 25 points in those three playoff losses.

I still remember Norman sitting in the stands alone after that 1990 wild-card loss to the Redskins at the Vet, after he had made the decision to fire Buddy. He looked like a basketball player with those long legs of his. He looked up at me and said, "Leo, I feel like I just got rid of the plague." Even with Buddy finally out of his hair, though, the thrill of owning the Eagles had started to fade for Norman. He always disputed the notion that he was vehemently disliked by Eagles fans. He insisted that whenever he walked around town when he flew up for games from his home in Miami Beach, people always were kind and gracious to him. But he knew better.

The long commutes from Florida also were starting to get old. When Jeffrey Lurie approached him about buying the team in the spring of 1994, and offered him nearly three times what he had paid for the team nine years earlier, Norman didn't have to think twice about selling.

I was sad when Norman sold the team. He had green-lighted my return to the Eagles in 1985 and treated me very well. At the time, I knew very little about Jeffrey and didn't know what to expect from him. But he quickly won me and the rest of the employees over. I so much enjoyed working for Jeffrey and former club president Joe Banner and the man who succeeded him, Don Smolenski. Don is a good friend. He's been with the organization since 1998, serving as the team's chief operating officer, chief financial officer and, since 2012, president. He's a first-round draft pick, a great businessman, and one of the good people.

Chapter 17
Buddy

Buddy Ryan was a real piece of work. The Frederick, Oklahoma, native had a perpetual chip on his shoulder. He was one of those guys who always clashed with authority, which enhanced his appeal with his players and the guy on the street. He didn't get along with Bears head coach Mike Ditka when he was the defensive coordinator there and, as discussed in the last chapter, he definitely didn't get along with Norman Braman and most of the other Eagles front-office executives after coming to Philadelphia.

The locker room, weight room, and coaching offices were in the basement of Veterans Stadium, while the executive offices were two floors up. Early on, Ryan created an us-versus-them mentality between the players and the coaches and the front office. He always referred to the Eagles' front office as "the third floor." That is, when he wasn't calling Braman "the man in France," or worse.

Ryan was an Oklahoma version of Mugs McGinnis, the pugnacious leader of the fictional Bowery Boys, played by Leo Gorcey. Buddy's players loved him. So did Eagles fans. Maybe he never managed to win a playoff game, but his Trump-like boastfulness and his willingness to openly disrespect the unpopular Braman every chance he got won him a spot in their hearts forever. Go figure.

Ryan used to do his weekly radio show at a Center City bar and restaurant called Rib-It. When Marion Campbell was the Eagles' head coach, almost nobody showed up for his radio shows except the people who happened already to be there eating dinner or having beers. In fact, Swampy would only answer questions that were submitted in advance and approved by the show's host, Merrill Reese.

Buddy's radio show, though, became one of the hottest tickets in town. Every week, the restaurant was packed to the gills. I'm talking standing room only. There would be people out on the sidewalk waiting to get in. When Buddy showed up, he'd get the kind of ovation usually reserved for a rock star. Ryan loved it. He loved being loved. These were his people. The former army platoon sergeant became a hero to Philly's blue-collar masses, while Braman became the antichrist.

You could see why many people liked Buddy. He did have many endearing qualities. But frankly he also could be a real asshole. I remember I once asked him to speak at St. Joe's Prep, my old high school. I picked him up right outside the stadium offices at the Vet. Not long after he got in my car, he reached under my seat, pulled out a bottle of scotch, and took a drink. I assure you I never carried alcohol in my car. To this day, I have no idea how he got it in there without me knowing about it, but he did.

Anyway, he was going to speak to the St. Joe's Prep Father's Club. Typically you would have maybe 12 fathers show up for one of those gatherings. When word got out that I was bringing Buddy, though, the place was jammed. There were people sitting on the stairs, on the windowsills, everywhere. When it was time for him to address the group, Buddy got up and said, in my mind, practically nothing. He acted bored to be there. But the fathers loved it; they gave him a standing ovation.

They would have Pepsi or Coke or ginger ale and ice on a table in the back of the room for these get-togethers. As we were getting ready to leave, Buddy grabbed a glass and only filled it with ice. When we got out to my car, he once again reached under the seat, grabbed the scotch bottle, and filled his glass. When we got back to the stadium, I turned to him and said, "Do me a favor, Buddy. Get the hell out of my car and take your booze with you and don't ever bring it back in here." He pretty much blew me off and said, "OK. See you tomorrow." That was Buddy.

I was a big racquetball guy in my younger days. I loved playing the game and became pretty good at it, if I do say so myself. I can't play anymore because of health issues, but back then I was still in good shape and I would play anybody. And I'd usually beat them. I played a lot with former Eagles players, such as John Bunting, Stan Walters, William Fuller, Chad Lewis, Mike Bartram, Mike Evans, Ron Jaworski, Bill Bergey, and many more. I also played against Buddy Ryan, but those games weren't very competitive; I could have beaten him with the racquet sticking out of my ear.

Jimmy Carr, who was a starting cornerback on the Eagles' 1960 NFL championship team and later was an assistant coach with the team in the early 1970s, actually was the guy who taught me how to play racquetball. Jimmy was quite a character. He would come into our offices and jump up on a desk and start dancing. It was hysterical. I remember this one girl we had working in the ticket office. She had just started with us and Jimmy came in and jumped up on her desk. She almost fainted.

We had a racquetball court in the basement of Veterans Stadium. Like I said, I was pretty good, and frankly I could be a little obnoxious. I loved talking trash after beating one of the players or coaches. I'd say, "You're a pro? I just kicked your ass." Well, Buddy eventually got tired of me doing that to him and his players and wanted to teach me a lesson. One day, I was in my office and Buddy called me and told me to come down to the court. He said he had a game for me. I told him I was really, really busy and wasn't sure I had the time. But he insisted.

This was before the start of the 1990 season, which would be Buddy's last with the Eagles. That summer, they had signed former Bears quarterback Jim McMahon to back up Randall Cunningham. When I got down to the racquetball court, McMahon was there with Buddy. I tried to strike up a conversation with McMahon. I said, "So do you play a lot, Jim?" He looked down at me, smiled, and said, "Sort of."

He said he played a lot when he was with the Bears. I asked him where he played in Chicago because I had played a little bit when I had visited there and thought maybe it was the same place he played. It wasn't. He said he played in his house. I thought, *Good Lord. The man has a racquetball court in his house. He can play anytime he wants.* I was beaten before he ever hit the first ball. I mean, I had never played against anyone who had his own racquetball court in his house. Jim was really, really good. He kicked my butt all over the place. After it was over, I came off the court, and there was Buddy, laughing hysterically. He looked at me and said, "You're not so hot now, are you, Carlin?"

That was the end of my ego trip with racquetball. But it was a great experience. Jim and I became friends and we played against each other often. He would always beat me, but it was enjoyable—and a little more competitive than that first ass kicking he gave me.

Another guy I used to play racquetball with a lot was Ken Iman. Ken—another good friend, who passed away in 2010 at the too-young age of 71—was a former NFL offensive lineman who played in the league for 14 years, most of them with the Los Angeles Rams. He was part of a great Rams offensive line that also included Hall of Famer Tom Mack, Joe Scibelli, Charlie Cowan, and Joe Carollo.

Ken played for Dick Vermeil when Vermeil was an assistant with the Rams under George Allen. When Vermeil got the Eagles' head coaching job in 1976, he asked Ken to join his staff as the offensive line coach. Iman coached the Eagles' offensive linemen for 10 years. He met his wife, Joyce, at Veterans Stadium. She was the Eagles' longtime accounting supervisor and spent almost as many years with the organization as me. After Buddy decided to replace Ken following the 1986 season, Norman Braman gave him a job in the sales and marketing department selling penthouse suites.

Anyway, Ken and I were playing racquetball one day down in the basement of the Vet when he accidentally took the top of my ear off with his racquet. It had to be sewn back on. I assure you, I handled it very well. OK, maybe not. I cried like a baby. The trainers weren't around, so Ken picked me up and carried me to his car and rushed me to the hospital. The team's orthopedic surgeon at the time, Dr. Vince DiStefano, was there. Ken had the wherewithal to put my ear on ice, and Vince sewed it back on.

Whenever anyone asked me how I was doing, I'd say "Sterling." Eventually, I put it on a sweater. But I wasn't sterling the day Ken Iman took a part of my ear off playing racquetball.

I remember asking him, "Hey, Vince. I'm not going to have any hearing problems, am I?" He started moving his lips and pretended to be talking. I was not amused. I called him a few choice names. But I'm eternally grateful to Vince. He did a nice job of saving the ear, and it has held steady ever since.

I continued to play racquetball after the ear episode, which wasn't the case with my rough-touch football career a few years earlier. That came to a sudden end after I broke my jaw playing and had to have it wired shut for six weeks. I remember when I got home after breaking it, one of our kids had a bump on his head from something and had an ice pack on the bump. I borrowed it and put it on my jaw in the hope that Kay wouldn't notice right away. When she realized what had happened, I thought she was going to kill me. Here we were with seven kids to feed and I'm out risking life and limb playing rough-touch football and getting hurt.

I went to work with the broken jaw. I saw our orthodontist, who confirmed it was broken. I couldn't yawn and couldn't eat solid food for six weeks while my jaw was wired shut. The worst part of it was the dental hygiene. I had to gargle every hour. I couldn't wait to get the wire out. What made the situation worse was the fact that the first doctor who wired my jaw did it improperly. Consequently, my jaw wasn't aligned the right way. When they realized it, they had to wire it a second time. Good God, that was torture.

Even after I broke my jaw, I wanted to keep playing. I brought a helmet home to see if wearing a face mask might protect it. When Kay realized what I was up to, she hit the roof and announced my retirement as a rough-touch player. "That's it. You're done," she said. I didn't argue. I couldn't have even if I had wanted to since I couldn't talk.

Getting back to Buddy Ryan, as I mentioned, he finally got fired after the 1990 season. The Eagles made the playoffs for the third straight year but also lost their one and only playoff game for the third straight year, which was more than enough reason for Norman to tell Buddy to hit the road. Norman considered Buddy's two coordinators—offensive coordinator Rich Kotite and defensive coordinator Jeff Fisher—as potential replacements. He ended up choosing Kotite.

Jeff was a terrific coach. He ended up spending nearly 20 years as a head coach with Houston/Tennessee and the St. Louis/Los Angeles Rams and was the longtime chairman of the league's competition committee. But Jeff had played for Buddy in Chicago and came to the Eagles with him as an assistant, and I think Norman just felt he was too closely aligned with Buddy to succeed him.

Kotite was a guy Norman knew he could get along with and someone who would never question him or give him the grief Buddy did. Rich was a fun guy. The Eagles won 10 games in his first year as head coach and 11 in his second, and even managed to do something Buddy couldn't—win a playoff game. They beat Jim Mora's Saints in a 1992 wild-card game. But Kotite was eventually fired by Lurie the year after Lurie bought the Eagles from Braman for $180 million.

Chapter 18

I Hope He's Faster Than His Old Man

This was the summer of 1986, Buddy Ryan's first training camp as the Eagles' head coach. Kay and I were out to dinner. When we came home, our youngest child, Carrie—my beautiful grand finale—ran up to us and said, "Dad, dad, dad. You have to call Joe Woolley. He needs to talk to you." Joe was the head of our player personnel department. Joe and I were friends, but I couldn't imagine what he needed to talk to me about. He was out in West Chester at the Eagles' training camp. In that thick Southern drawl of his, Joe said, "Buddy wants your son Leo in camp at 8:00 tomorrow morning."

Leo had graduated from Holy Cross a couple months earlier. He was a very good wide receiver there. He was the team's leading receiver, captain of the team, and all of that good stuff, but he wasn't really considered a pro prospect. He hadn't been drafted or signed by anyone as a free agent. But injuries at wide receiver and a holdout by the team's star wide receiver, Mike Quick, had left the Eagles shorthanded at the position in camp.

It was pretty exciting that they wanted to bring in Leo. There was only one problem: we couldn't find him. He was out enjoying his postgraduation freedom before having to get a job in the real world.

Leo Jr. at Eagles training camp in 1986. The Eagles signed him after camp holdouts left them short of wideouts.

Translation: he was out at some local watering hole and didn't get home until really late. I went up to him when he came in the door and said, "Guess what, buddy? You're going to be trying out for the Eagles." He looked at me in disbelief.

I didn't go to training camp much in those days. Training camp is great for the fans—they love it—but I had too much to do in the office. But you can bet I was there that day. I wouldn't have missed it for the world. Leo managed to get a few hours sleep and got dressed, then I drove him out to West Chester to the Eagles' training camp to take his physical. The next thing I knew, my boy was running out on the field in a green-and-white uniform, which is something I had dreamed of doing since I was a kid in North Philly. Unfortunately, for me it was a pipe dream. But there was Leo, out there with the 100-plus other Eagles campers. I was beaming with pride.

He wanted to play so badly that when he was getting his physical and the doctor asked him if he had ever had any operations, he said no. The doctor gave him a curious look and said, "Hmm. Then what'd you get that scar on your knee from?" Leo had hurt his knee in high school and had surgery on it. It had long ago healed, though, and they cleared him.

Ray Didinger, a longtime Philadelphia sportswriter who was working for the *Philadelphia Daily News* at the time, came up to me. He said, "What are you doing here? You don't usually come out to camp." I said, "You're not gonna believe what I'm doing here." Then I pointed out to the field and said, "They signed my son." A couple minutes later, reporters and photographers were all around us. I still remember the first paragraph of one of the stories in the papers the next day: "Is there enough room for two Leo Carlins on one football team?" It was a blast.

Both Leo and I knew his chances of making the team weren't very good. But that was OK. He wasn't the biggest kid in the world, but what God didn't give him in size, he gave him in toughness. He typified the saying that it's not the size of the dog in the fight, it's the size of the fight in the dog.

Toward the end of camp, Quick, a longtime friend and the Eagles' radio analyst for the last two decades, finally reported, and that was the end of Leo's professional football career. It was one of the greatest experiences of his life, though. He had a lot of fun and made a lot of friends on the team. He still kids around with Quick about not holding out of camp long enough.

Leo played in all of the team's preseason games that season, and he gave it everything he had. I was very proud of him. Many of the coaches came up to me and told me how impressed they were with the amount of drive Leo had for somebody his size.

I remember the first preseason game that Leo played in that summer, against either Detroit or San Diego. I was back home in Philly watching the game on TV. The late, great Stu Nahan was doing the play-by-play, and Dick Vermeil was handling the color commentary.

Stu, who passed away in 2007, has a star on the Hollywood Walk of Fame. He is remembered primarily for his work as a broadcaster in Los Angeles and for being the fight commentator in the first five *Rocky* movies, but he spent time in Philly early in his career. He was a star hockey goalie at McGill University in Montreal and spent a few years in the Toronto Maple Leafs organization. Later he was the Flyers' play-by-play guy in their first few years of existence and also hosted a children's show called *Captain Philadelphia* on a Philly TV station. In it he dressed up as an astronaut. Seriously.

Anyway, when Leo got into the game for the first time in that preseason game, Stu said, "Into the game comes Leo Carlin, wide receiver from Holy Cross." To which Vermeil said, "Leo Carlin? Geez, I hope he's faster than his old man."

He definitely was. And still is.

Chapter 19
Job Offers

During my long career with the Eagles, I occasionally received job offers from other teams. One of those was from the Miami Dolphins and their owner, Joe Robbie. It was in the early 1970s. The season was over, and he had someone from the Dolphins organization call me and invite me down to South Florida. It was cold and snowing in Philadelphia when I boarded the flight to Miami. When I got off the plane, the weather was absolutely perfect. That kind of weather can cloud your judgment.

I was taken to meet Mr. Robbie, who was a very dynamic man with a huge capacity for work. We talked for probably two hours. At the end of the interview, he offered me the job but told me I had to give him an answer by Monday. It was Thursday. I called a friend of mine who was an assistant coach with the Dolphins and asked him for his advice. He told me to get on the plane and go back to Philadelphia and not to look back.

Apparently there were a lot of problems in the organization at the time that you couldn't see from the outside. Robbie and his coach, Don Shula, didn't particularly like one another. But Shula was a future Hall of Fame coach and Robbie wasn't going to fire him, no matter how much he wanted to. A day later, I called Mr. Robbie and told him I was going to stay put.

I also had an opportunity to move to Detroit in 1973 and work for the Lions. Russ Thomas was the Lions' general manager. He called our GM at the time, Pete Retzlaff, to get permission to talk to me. Pete was a good friend of mine right up until his death in 2020. Pete gave Russ permission to talk to me, and I went out there to interview. I remember taking a cab from the airport to the Lions' offices. As we were going down this busy street, I looked to my right. I asked the cabbie what that was off in the distance. He said it was Canada. Right then and there I pretty much decided I wasn't going to be taking that job. It was cold enough in Philadelphia. And being a Philly kid, I wasn't crazy about living on the Canadian border.

Even though I already had decided there was no way in hell I was taking the job, I went through with the interview, and it actually went great. They needed somebody with ticketing experience, particularly somebody who had experience with a stadium move. They were building a new stadium—the Silverdome—out in suburban Pontiac, about 30 miles from downtown. They had been sharing a downtown stadium with Detroit's baseball team, the Tigers, since 1938.

While I was there, I bumped into Eddie Khayat, who had played for the Eagles in the late 1950s and early '60s when I first started working there, and who had been fired as the Eagles' head coach a year earlier by Leonard. Eddie, who now was an assistant coach with the Lions, and I were good friends. He put the full-court press on me, telling me what a terrific organization the Lions had. He was very persuasive, but I'm a Philly kid and turned the Lions down.

Three other teams—the Jets, the Patriots, and the Saints—also came knocking. I was flattered that they thought so highly of me. The Patriots' offer came from Upton Bell, the son of former NFL commissioner Bert Bell, who was the Patriots' GM at the time. This was roughly around the same time as the Lions' offer. I had helped the Eagles become the first NFL team to merge ticketing with computer technology, and other teams were intrigued.

The Saints' offer was interesting. Kay and I flew down there and were put up in an expensive hotel and wined and dined by Saints executives, who even told us about the local Jesuit schools we could send our sons to. It was very nice. But like said, I'm a Philly kid.

Chapter 20
The Parade of Coaches

Coaches are a different breed. They work hard and make a lot of money, but I often wonder whether it's worth it. They are hired to be fired and move around like gypsies, particularly early in their careers. It wreaks havoc on their family. Having a coach in my own family—my son Clayton—I understand what they go through. It's difficult.

In the more than 50 years I spent in professional football, I worked with 14 different head coaches and God knows how many assistant coaches. Of those 14 head coaches—13 with the Eagles, plus the Stars' Jim Mora—only four lasted more than four years: Joe Kuharich (5), Dick Vermeil (7), Buddy Ryan (5), and Andy Reid (14).

The first coach I worked with was Buck Shaw, who coached the Eagles' 1960 championship team. Buck was a stately looking gray-haired man. He was so distinguished-looking that if you didn't know who he was, you never would've guessed he was a football coach.

Shaw played three years for Knute Rockne at Notre Dame before getting into coaching. He had been Air Force's head coach before the Eagles hired him in 1958. He stayed around just three years, retiring after they won the 1960 title. It's not easy walking away from a championship team, but he did it. He was only 60 when he retired. He moved to California, where he had spent a significant chunk of his coaching career

(Santa Clara University, the University of California, the San Francisco 49ers) and became an executive for a paper products company.

Next came Nick Skorich. Nick was kind of an aloof guy; he kept to himself much of the time. His Eagles went 10–4 the year after they won the championship, then everything kind of went to hell. They won just three games in 1962 and two in 1963, and Jerry Wolman fired Skorich.

Wolman replaced Skorich with Joe Kuharich, who, as I mentioned earlier, might've been the most unpopular coach I've ever been associated with. As the team's business manager back then as well as the ticket manager, I was in charge of a lot of our advertising. I remember one of the banks in Philly wanted to run an ad that said, "How would you like a 15-year no-cut contract?" That, of course, was a reference to the 15-year contract Wolman had given Kuharich. I had to turn that one down. But that was the kind of thing people were doing when Joe was the head coach.

Leonard Tose fired Kuharich right after he bought the team from Wolman in 1969. At the advice of his new GM, Pete Retzlaff, he replaced Joe with Jerry Williams. Jerry had played for the Eagles as a receiver for a couple years in 1953 and 1954. He was a player-coach on the 1954 team. He coached the team's defensive backs from 1957 through 1963, when Retzlaff was the team's tight end, so they were friends.

Williams's hiring turned out to be another disaster. We won just 7 of 31 games with Williams as the head coach. Leonard was embarrassed by the display of talent on the field. He thought that with a new coach and new approach to the game, we should have been a lot better. He fired Jerry just three games into the 1971 season. Three games! I'm not sure, but that may be an NFL record for the earliest head coaching firing ever.

Leonard replaced Williams with my good friend Eddie Khayat. Eddie was a starting defensive tackle on the Eagles' 1960 championship team. He brought a fresh approach to things; he wanted his players to be disciplined. He issued a mandate once banning all facial hair. Keep in mind this was the late 1960s and early '70s, when facial hair—particularly mustaches—was very popular. We had a bunch of guys with mustaches, and they all had to shave them off. Many of the players resented it. Eddie might've had the most clean-shaven team in the league, but he didn't make any friends in the locker room with that edict.

One of the guys on that team was a linebacker by the name of Tim Rossovich. Tim was quite a character. He did some truly crazy things, including setting himself on fire once and eating glass. That's right, eating glass. Tim had a Fu Manchu mustache that he was quite proud of. Eddie made him get rid of it. Tim managed to make a profit doing it, however. He got a commercial endorsement from a shaving cream company to shave off the mustache on camera.

The Eagles went a respectable 6–4–1 after Eddie took over for Williams in 1971 but finished 2–11–1 in '72. The offense, with John Reaves and Pete Liske at quarterback, was awful. They scored more than 12 points only four times during the entire season. Eddie was funny, hardworking, and dedicated, but he never had a chance. Leonard tired of him quickly and fired him at the end of that dreadful 1972 season. The players were happy; they got to grow their mustaches and beards back.

After Khayat came Mike McCormack, a big, burly former offensive lineman. He was another hardworking, likeable guy. We got him from the Washington Redskins, where he had worked under George Allen. He decided to go the "future is now" route like Allen did in Washington, trading away draft picks to get veteran players who would help him win right away. Or at least that was the idea. The problem was, the veteran players McCormack gave up all those draft picks for weren't very good. The "future is now" plan didn't work. I don't pretend to be an expert, but sometimes you've got to build. It was another disaster.

Mike and I used to play racquetball together. We'd be doubles partners and looked absolutely ridiculous—Mutt and Jeff. There'd be me and Mike, who was an offensive tackle for the Browns, against two of Mike's assistants—6'7" former Packers receiver Boyd Dowler and John Sandusky, another former offensive lineman. You couldn't even find me in there on the court with those guys. It was a wonder I didn't get my head knocked off.

Once when McCormack was the head coach, Leonard decided he was going to call a play. He called all of the team's male personnel into his office one day for a meeting, including Mike and his coaches. That's right, none of the women in the organization were invited to the meeting. Leonard felt women were good for only one thing, and it wasn't drawing up football plays. Leonard told everybody he wanted to see more life on the field. It had to be very embarrassing for McCormack, with his whole staff standing there with him. During the course of the meeting, Leonard said, "By the way, I have this play I want you to run." The irony of the whole thing was that we had just hired Johnny Rauch, who was supposed to be one of the leading offensive minds in football. And here was our owner telling him what to run.

Harold Carmichael was our best wide receiver at the time. He also had a helluva arm; he could throw the ball a mile. Leonard's suggestion was to have the quarterback hand the ball off to Harold on an apparent end-around. Meanwhile, our tight end, Charle Young, would run down the field and wave his arm and Harold would throw the ball to him. That was the play.

Well, Sunday came, and we were in the press box at Veterans Stadium for the game when the buzz started. Everybody was saying, "Here comes the play, here comes the play." We knew when it was coming because Leonard also told McCormack *when* to call the play. Can you imagine that being done today? Well, OK, but can you imagine it being done anywhere besides Dallas? Anyway, the play was a complete flop. I don't think Harold's throw ever reached Charle. The fans got a good laugh out of it at least.

McCormack's 1974 team actually managed to finish 7–7, but they won only four games the next year and Leonard fired McCormack after the '75 season. That's when Leonard made one of the few smart moves of his entire ownership. He pursued and hired a young, charismatic college coach from UCLA by the name of Dick Vermeil.

Dick had been an outstanding special teams coach with the Rams and had spent the previous two years as the head coach at UCLA. In 1975, while the Eagles were stumbling to a 4–10 record, Vermeil's Bruins went 9–2–1, won their first conference championship in a decade, and upset No. 1–ranked Ohio State in the Rose Bowl. Leonard courted him and made Dick an offer he couldn't refuse.

With Dick Vermeil.

The Eagles team Dick took over not only wasn't very good, it also didn't have any draft ammunition to get better, thanks to McCormack's failed "future is now" strategy. Keep in mind this was long before the advent of free agency. The only way to improve your team back then was through the draft or trades. The Eagles had no picks in the first three rounds of the 1976 draft, they didn't have any picks in the first *four* rounds of the 1977 draft, and they didn't have a first- or second-round pick in the 1978 draft. It wasn't until 1979, Dick's fourth year in Philly, that he finally had a first-round pick. But that didn't stop him. In 1978, even without the benefit of good draft position, the Eagles made the playoffs. They made it to the postseason again in 1979, and in 1980 they beat the Dallas Cowboys in the NFC Championship Game and made it to the Super Bowl.

In the process, however, Dick nearly worked himself to death. He worked 20-hour days and often slept in his office during the season. By 1982 he was burned out and walked away from coaching. He became a very successful broadcaster and eventually returned to coaching 15 years later with the St. Louis Rams and won a Super Bowl with them. When Dick first took the Rams job, he drove his players hard in training camp, much like he had when he coached the Eagles two decades earlier. But times had changed and Dick faced a lot of pushback from his players. They finally convinced him to take his foot off the gas a little, and everybody lived happily ever after.

After he won the Super Bowl with the Rams, Dick retired again for a year before accepting his longtime friend Carl Peterson's offer to coach the Kansas City Chiefs. He spent five years in Kansas City. He won 13 games one year there and 10 another year. He was a finalist for the Hall of Fame this year and hopefully will eventually get in, because I know how much it would mean to him.

Aside from being a great coach, Dick is one of the finest men I've ever known. If I had been big enough and fast enough to play football at the pro level, I would have wanted to play for Dick. He drove his players

Attending a police charity function with Dick Vermeil (third from right) in 1977.

hard, but they loved him. All of the players who played for him were fiercely loyal to him and would do anything for him; they still would. Dick hosts a golf outing every year for the Boy Scouts of America, and his former players come in from all over the country to attend it simply because Dick asks them. He holds a fund-raising dinner or a reunion, and everybody comes—no matter how far away they live, no matter what else they've got going on—because they know Dick would do the same thing for them.

Dick's capacity to be a friend is limitless. He financially supported Tose after he went broke and has helped many of his former teammates when they've been down on their luck financially. Even today, nearly 40 years after he last coached a game for the Eagles, he still is extremely popular in Philadelphia. I've met few people in this world more likeable and more loyal than Dick. He was kind enough to come to my retirement party in 2015, and I'll never forget him for it. He's one of the finest men ever to come through the Eagles organization. The fact that Leonard brought him in just goes to show you that even a blind squirrel can occasionally stumble upon an acorn.

Marion Campbell, another member of the Eagles' 1960 championship team, who had been Vermeil's defensive coordinator, replaced his boss as head coach in 1983. Campbell had been the Atlanta Falcons' head coach for three years in the mid-1970s; he won only six games in those three years.

He was a nice man and a terrific defensive coordinator. Maybe with the right talent he would have been a good head coach. But he inherited an aging team from Vermeil and never won more than six games in any of his three seasons with the Eagles.

Buddy Ryan came next. To his credit, Buddy did manage to turn the Eagles around. They made the playoffs his last three years, but he was 0–3 in the postseason despite having one of the league's best defenses and a difference-making quarterback. Norman Braman had been looking for a reason to fire Buddy almost from the day he made the mistake of hiring him. Buddy's failure in the postseason ended up being more than enough.

Braman replaced Ryan with Rich Kotite, who had been Buddy's offensive coordinator in 1990 after four years in the same position with the New York Jets. With Randall Cunningham at quarterback, Kotite's offense had flourished in Ryan's final season as head coach in 1990. The Eagles finished third in total offense and third in scoring that year. With Randall rushing for more than 900 yards, they finished first in rushing. His 30 touchdown passes were the second-most in the league that year (Warren Moon threw 33). He also ran for five touchdowns.

But Kotite's offense came up small in the playoffs that year and went one-and-done in the postseason, losing at home to the Redskins 20–6. Cunningham rushed for 80 yards but completed only 15 of 29 passes and failed to throw a touchdown pass in the playoffs for the third straight year.

Ryan's defensive coordinator, Jeff Fisher, probably would have been the wiser choice to replace Ryan. He certainly went on to enjoy greater success and longevity as an NFL head coach. But as I mentioned earlier, Fisher had played for Buddy in Chicago and was considered a "Buddy guy." After five combative years with Ryan, Norman just wanted a head coach he could trust and who would do what he asked. That was Kotite.

I liked Rich. He was a very friendly guy. He lost Randall to a season-ending knee injury in his first game as head coach in 1991, but his team still won 10 games that season and almost made the playoffs. He did make the playoffs in 1992 and '93, but then Norman sold the team to Jeffrey Lurie in April 1994, and that was the beginning of the end for Rich.

He didn't make a very good early impression on Lurie. The new owner caught him sneaking out of the Vet with his golf clubs one afternoon before the 1994 draft. Rich loved to play golf; he still does. And the fact that the Eagles' first-round pick in that draft—offensive tackle Bernard Williams—ended up preferring marijuana to football, and that their second-round pick—defensive tackle Bruce Walker—had been arrested in college for stealing stereos and computer equipment, didn't help Kotite any. Still, the Eagles ended up winning seven of their first nine games in '94. When Lurie declined to give Kotite a vote of confidence on whether he'd be back the following year, an insulted Kotite said he was going to do "some evaluating of [his] own."

That, of course, ended up backfiring, because the Eagles followed that 7–2 start with an epic collapse, losing their final seven games. Cunningham followed his 30-touchdown season under Kotite with one of the poorest years of his career. He threw just 16 touchdown passes and 13 interceptions. By mid-December, Kotite benched him in favor of Bubby Brister. That's right, Bubby Brister!

After buying the Eagles, Lurie tried to use the league's more successful teams as guideposts for how he wanted to run the Eagles and build his roster. There was no more successful a team in the league at the time than the San Francisco 49ers, who had just won their third Super Bowl in seven years. Lurie and Joe Banner spent a lot of time picking the brains of 49ers owner Eddie DeBartolo and his club president, Carmen Policy. When Lurie fired Kotite one day after the 1994 season ended, he even hired someone from the 49ers organization—their defensive coordinator, Ray Rhodes.

Ray grew up on the mean streets of Mexia, Texas. A 10th-round pick of the Giants in 1974, he initially was a wide receiver who was later switched to cornerback. He was a hard-nosed player who managed to carve out a respectable seven-year career in the league.

He was a different kind of guy. I worked out every day and would be in the locker room a lot and got to know him pretty well. I happened to be in the shower one day when Ray was in there and he confessed to me that he'd rather be an assistant coach than a head coach. He wasn't kidding. He didn't like the responsibility, the pressure, and the attention that came with being a head coach. He just liked coaching football. I'm sure he liked the fact that he made a lot more money as a head coach, but that might've been the only thing he liked about it.

Ray hated to lose. I mean, he really hated it. I remember once, at a press conference the day after the Eagles lost a game at home, he stood in front of a roomful of reporters and cameras and compared the defeat to having someone break into his house, rob him, and sodomize his wife and daughters. Boy, did he catch a hundred kinds of hell for that, including from his wife and daughters. But that was Ray. He was as unvarnished as they came; what you saw was what you got.

On the sideline before every game, Ray used to reach into his pocket and pull out an ammonia tablet—aka smelling salts—break it in half, put it under his nose, and inhale. Smelling salts are often used on athletes who have been dazed or knocked unconscious to wake them up. And for decades, NFL players have used them as a stimulant before games. Michael Strahan, the former Giants Hall of Fame defensive end, estimated once that 70 to 80 percent of the players in the league used smelling salts, which aren't banned by the league. But Rhodes was the only coach I ever knew who used them.

We had some success in Ray's first couple of years with the Eagles. We made the playoffs in 1995 and '96. But we finished 6–9–1 in 1997. After we started 0–5 in 1998, it was game, set, and match for Ray. He knew he was a dead man walking. Funny thing is, after that reality set in with him, that's probably as calm as I ever saw him. He seemed fine with it, almost relieved—like a guy in quicksand being thrown a rope.

Ray was one of the few coaches I ever knew—Buddy Ryan was another—who never was going to work himself to death. Ray never was tempted to sleep in his office like Vermeil.

Chapter 21

Big Red

Jeff Lurie's next hire—Andy Reid—turned out to be one of the smartest decisions he's ever made. The decision came down to two men—Reid, who was the Green Bay Packers' quarterbacks coach at the time—and Pittsburgh Steelers defensive coordinator Jim Haslett.

Tom Modrak, who had been hired by Lurie as the team's director of football operations the previous year, clearly favored Haslett. Modrak had been a longtime personnel man with the Steelers and knew Haslett well. Modrak and Haslett also had both attended the same college— Indiana University of Pennsylvania—though not at the same time.

Haslett was the known. He had three years of experience as an NFL coordinator—one with New Orleans in 1996 and two with the Steelers. Reid was unknown. He had never been a coordinator at any level.

Tom liked Reid OK but wasn't sure whether he was ready to make the giant leap from a position coach to a head job. Hell, Tom wasn't the only one who wondered about that. There were nine head coaching openings after the 1998 season. The Eagles were the only one of the nine teams looking for a head coach that saw fit to interview Reid.

The Packers, for whom Reid had worked for the previous eight years, were one of the teams shopping for a new head coach that year. Their coach, Mike Holmgren, had left to become coach and general manager of the Seattle Seahawks. But Packers general manager Ron Wolf, who was inducted into the Pro Football Hall of Fame in 2018, never bothered to interview Reid. To this day, almost every head coach who has been hired in the NFL either had previous NFL coordinator experience or had been a head coach in college or somewhere else in the league. Reid obviously had neither. Ironically, Wolf ended up hiring the guy we had just fired, Rhodes. Ray lasted just one year in Green Bay before Wolf fired him. Wolf has said he always believed Andy was going to be a good head coach; he just didn't think he was ready. He told Jeffrey he didn't think it was "his time yet."

Jeffrey and Joe Banner looked at it differently. They felt that, given how hard it is to find a good coach, if you are firmly convinced someone is going to be a great coach in a year or two—and they believed that about Reid—grab him. Few head coaches back then—regardless of experience—were turning around teams in their first year anyway, so they didn't see it as a big sacrifice to hire someone such as Andy, who might not be the best he could be until his second or third year. Lurie and Banner were so impressed with Reid that they offered him the job.

"It obviously was a leap of faith because you never know," Lurie said. "But Andy exhibited so many wonderful qualities of loving the game and being so curious to advance his own state of knowledge in every way possible and wanting to establish a culture where there was serious dedication and attention to detail."

Lurie added, "He loved game planning and everything that went into that. He was respectful of people. All the things that we wanted to make sure were embedded in the culture of the team and the franchise. And that was just the tip of the iceberg. He really exhibited an obsession for doing things right."

Lurie had a little bit of inside information that helped ease his mind about hiring Reid. While Wolf may not have believed Reid was ready, Mike Holmgren did. Holmgren told Jeffrey that, while Andy's title with the Packers may not have been coordinator, he was so involved in their game planning and play calling that he essentially was the team's offensive coordinator.

Reid's obsession for detail and planning was evident when he showed up at his interview with a dictionary-sized notebook. "The book had everything you could possibly imagine if you were preparing yourself to become a head coach in the NFL," Banner said. "He literally had things like notes from speeches that other head coaches had given on opening day. . . . The thing that maybe was most impressive to us was he had ranked every coach at every single position 1 through 10, including college guys. He literally had a draft board of coaches. He would have a wide receiver coach as the sixth-rated guy and you'd ask him why he was No. 6, and the extent of detail and insight he showed in answering those questions was really stunning. To this day, I've seen nothing like it from any other coach." The book gave Lurie and Banner confidence that Reid could evaluate coaches and put together a solid staff and manage it, which they felt was critical.

While Reid may have made a few staff missteps later on in his 14-year tenure in Philly, his early coaching hires were generally exceptional. He hired two experienced hands as coordinators—Rod Dowhower as his offensive coordinator and the late Jim Johnson as his defensive lieutenant. Ten of his assistants have gone on to be NFL head coaches.

"It was more important how Andy talked about how he intended to run things as head coach and what he was going to be looking for in his coaches and why he was going to be looking for that and how he was going to mesh older coaches with younger coaches than it was to have actual names," Banner said. "Our feeling was if we couldn't trust him to pick an offensive or defensive coordinator, we shouldn't be hiring him as head coach. If he has the right thought process and has done the right work and recognizes how important that hire is, then we should trust him and get out of the way and let him do it. And that's what we did."

Reid spent 14 years as the Eagles' head coach. It was the longest tenure of any coach in the franchise's history. His teams won 130 games, made the playoffs nine times, won six NFC East titles, and advanced to the NFC Championship Game five times. What Andy didn't do in those 14 years, unfortunately, was win a Super Bowl. The Eagles lost four of the five conference championship games they played in. The only one they won was in 2004, but they lost to Bill Belichick and the Patriots in Super Bowl XXXIX.

Because he never won a Super Bowl in Philly, Andy never was fully appreciated by Eagles fans. They constantly booed him and insulted him with comments about his weight or his clock management or something else. Every year, even when the Eagles made the playoffs, the people on talk radio would be calling for his firing.

I like Andy a lot; he's a good man. We are friends. We used to play racquetball together. He dealt with some difficult personal issues during his time in Philly, none more tragic than the death of his son Garrett in 2012. Garrett, who had a history of drug problems, died from a heroin overdose. He was found in his room at Lehigh University, where the Eagles trained back then. Garrett had been helping the team's equipment and training staffs during camp.

Andy tried to deal with Garrett's death and keep coaching; he didn't take any time off. Maybe he should have, because he clearly was distracted and it ended up having a trickle-down effect on his team. The Eagles finished 4–12 that year and missed the playoffs for the second straight year.

Jeffrey loved Andy a lot and didn't want to fire him. But by the end of the 2012 season, both of them knew it was time for a change. I've had a front-row seat for a lot of firings during my years with the Eagles, but none was as—for lack of a better word—nice as Andy's. It was more like a retirement celebration than a firing. The day they parted ways, Jeffrey had a reception for Andy in the cafeteria at the NovaCare Complex. The cafeteria staff had baked a big cake. Jeffrey gave Andy a football that was signed by everyone in the organization. They embraced. Reid was given a standing ovation by everyone in the room. A lot of tears were shed that day.

After 14 years with the Eagles, I thought Andy would take some time off after he left Philadelphia to spend time with his family and cope with Garrett's death, but I was wrong. Andy felt the best medicine for dealing with his grief was to keep coaching. Four days after he walked out of the NovaCare Complex, he was hired by the Kansas City Chiefs to be their head coach.

He repeated the success he had with the Eagles in KC. The Chiefs made the playoffs in six of his first seven seasons there, and on February 2, 2020, in his 21st year as an NFL head coach, Andy finally got to hoist the Lombardi Trophy when his Chiefs beat the San Francisco 49ers in Super Bowl LIV. Jeffrey seldom attends Super Bowls that the Eagles aren't in, but he was in Miami to watch Reid finally land his white whale. The two remained close after Reid left Philadelphia.

I was so happy watching the Chiefs win the Super Bowl. Andy is the seventh-winningest head coach in NFL history, but all you would ever hear from his critics was that he couldn't win the big one. Well, he's finally put an end to that talk.

Andy is only 61, and he's got one of the best young quarterbacks in the game playing for him—24-year-old Patrick Mahomes. With Mahomes there, I don't see Big Red retiring anytime soon. Within the next two or three years, he figures to move up to No. 4 on the all-time wins list. Even if he doesn't manage to win another Super Bowl, he's a lock to make the Hall of Fame after he retires. Nobody deserves it more.

After Lurie let Reid go, he decided to again do a little outside-the-box thinking as far as a replacement. He hired an innovative college coach, the University of Oregon's Chip Kelly. Kelly had taken the Ducks to national prominence. He ran a no-huddle, hurry-up offense that exhausted defenses and piled up points. Kelly had no NFL experience, but the gamble seemed to pay off when Kelly's first team went 10–6 and made the playoffs and his second team also won 10 games.

But Chip had a really weird personality. I mentioned earlier that the man who replaced Buck Shaw in 1961—Nick Skorich—was aloof. Well, compared to Chip, Nick was a real people person. Kelly would pass you in the hall at the NovaCare Complex and not even make eye contact. He didn't really have any kind of relationship with his players, and he seldom was interested in communicating with Lurie or the team's general manager, Howie Roseman.

Roseman was instrumental in Kelly's hiring, but after the 2014 season, Kelly basically told Lurie that he needed to have absolute power over all personnel decisions and couldn't work with Howie. Lurie gave Kelly the power he requested and moved Roseman to a lesser role. But it didn't take Jeffrey long to regret his decision. He ended up firing Kelly late in the 2015 season.

After Lurie fired Chip Kelly, he turned to Reid for help in finding a replacement. Reid evaluated all of the replacement candidates Jeffrey was considering, including Doug Pederson, who had been a player and an assistant on Andy's staff in Philadelphia and was his offensive coordinator in Kansas City. Lurie hired Pederson on Andy's recommendation.

Chapter 22
Wheeling and Dealing

I've known Rich Gannon since he was a teenager. Three of my sons played football with him at St. Joe's Prep. He and Clayton were in the same grade and have been lifelong friends. Rich was a terrific kid who turned into an even better man. He always has been a high-character person. My family loves him. He's like a nephew to Kay and me. As a kid, he spent a lot of time around our house and would even go down the shore with us on vacation. I used to find him asleep on our couch some mornings when I'd get up.

My kids were pretty good players, but Rich was in a different stratosphere talent-wise. He excelled in several sports but particularly football. He played quarterback at the University of Delaware for the late, great Tubby Raymond and broke 21 school records. He was drafted by the New England Patriots in the fourth round of the 1987 NFL Draft. Getting drafted by an NFL team is supposed to be one of the most exciting days in a player's life, but it wasn't for Rich. He wasn't happy at all when the Patriots selected him. Rich wanted to play quarterback in the NFL, but the Patriots didn't view him as a quarterback; they drafted him with the idea of converting him to defensive back.

Rich called me after he got drafted and told me that I would never see him in a Patriots uniform. He said he would go to law school if he couldn't get the opportunity to play quarterback in the NFL. He asked me if there was anything I could do. Player personnel wasn't exactly my area of expertise. I was a ticket guy and wasn't sure how I could help him, but I love Rich and would do anything for him so I said I'd see what I could do.

I found out the Minnesota Vikings, who picked two spots after the Patriots, had wanted to draft Rich. And unlike the Patriots, they wanted to keep him at quarterback, not move him to the other side of the ball.

One of the Patriots' top executives at the time was Bucko Kilroy, who I knew a little bit. Bucko, like me, was a Philly kid, though a bit older. Bucko, who died in 2007 at the age of 86, grew up in Port Richmond and went to high school at Northeast Catholic. He spent 13 years playing in the NFL, all of them with the Eagles. He was a member of their 1948 and 1949 NFL title teams. During his career, he developed a reputation for being one of the league's dirtiest players, a reputation he relished. After he retired, he spent four years as an assistant coach with the Eagles and another two as a scout in 1960 and 1961, after I joined the Eagles' ticket department. Bucko later worked as a scout with the Cowboys and Redskins before joining the Patriots in 1971 as their player personnel boss. He ended up spending 35 years with the Patriots in various roles, including as their general manager from 1979 to 1982 and as team vice president from 1983 to 1993.

After the draft, I called Bucko. I was nervous about making the call because, like I said, personnel wasn't my area of expertise and the Eagles weren't even involved in this situation. I asked Bucko if the Patriots would be willing to make a deal with the Vikings, maybe do something along the lines of a future trade that would give Rich a chance to chase his quarterback dream.

He said to me, "Oh yeah, the kid from St. Joe's Prep. I hear he wants to be a quarterback." Bucko also knew that Rich probably wasn't going to sign with the Patriots if they were going to switch him to defense. I said, "If you make a deal with Minnesota, you'd be saving yourself a draft pick and both sides would walk away happy."

He said, "Let me ask you a question, Leo." Well, now I was really panicking. I was thinking he was going to ask me a football question like "How does he throw the out route?" or "What's his drop-back time?" or something like that, which no ticket director knows well enough to tell an experienced personnel guy such as Bucko. But he didn't ask me a football question. He asked me what Philadelphia parish Rich was from. That's a typical Philadelphia question in the Catholic world of our city. I honestly wasn't sure. I could have mentioned one of a dozen different parishes; I went with St. Leo's just for the heck of it. It was in Northeast Philly, just five miles from Bucko's parish, St. Anne's. It must have been the right answer, because six days later, Rich was a Viking. I was forever grateful to Bucko for doing that. That was the one and only trade of my career. But I tell everybody that when it comes to trades, I'm batting 1.000. One-for-one.

Rich, of course, went on to play quarterback in the NFL for 17 years with four teams—the Vikings (6), Redskins (1), Chiefs (4), and Raiders (6). He threw for nearly 29,000 yards, earned four Pro Bowl invitations, and was the league's Most Valuable Player in 2002 when he led the Raiders to the Super Bowl. For the last 14 years, he's been a game analyst for CBS. Most important, he's one of the finest individuals I've ever met, and I'm proud to call him my friend.

Rich, Clayton, and I usually get together at least once during the summer, if not more. We go to church and have breakfast together. He's a true friend. It was great to have been nominated for the Pro Football Hall of Fame with him.

A while back, he built a house in Ocean City, New Jersey, and he called me. He said, "I've plopped at your house so many times. Anytime you want to use my house, it's yours. You can have it." That's the kind of guy Rich is.

Chapter 23
The Ultimate Weapon

Randall Cunningham was one of the most exciting players in Eagles history. He had a rifle for an arm and could run like the wind. He was a legitimate double threat. Actually, he was a triple threat considering he could also punt. In fact, his 91-yard punt in 1989 still is the longest in franchise history. He also had an 80-yarder a few years later.

Randall had 207 career touchdown passes and threw for nearly 30,000 yards. He also rushed for nearly 5,000 yards, including 500-plus yards six times in his first seven seasons in the league. *Sports Illustrated* put him on their cover once and labeled him "The Ultimate Weapon." Hard to disagree with that.

Randall was an interesting guy. He fancied himself more than just a football player. He liked to hobnob with celebrities. He dated Whitney Houston for a little while, but she preferred the "bad boy" type. One time, he and a couple of his teammates—I believe it was running back Keith Byars and tight end Keith Jackson—got permission from Buddy Ryan to leave a preseason game early so they could drive up to New York City for Whitney's birthday party. When he built his first house, he even named one of the bedrooms after her. The White House has the Lincoln bedroom; Randall's mansion had the Whitney Houston bedroom. Sadly, Whitney died in 2012 at the too-young age of 48.

Early in his Eagles career, a local television station approached Randall about having his own weekly TV show during the season. He was gung ho about the idea but didn't want it to be the usual kind of boring X's-and-O's, let's-review-the-film-of-last-week's-game football show. He wanted to do the show like Arsenio Hall, with a band and guests and a live studio audience—the works. Amazingly, the station agreed. It actually ended up being a neat idea. At least I thought so.

Randall did everything in a big way. That included his wedding. In May 1993 he married Felicity De Jager, a professional dancer with the famous Dance Theatre of Harlem. His wedding was slightly bigger than the one Kay and I had in 1959. Actually, it was bigger than *any* wedding I had ever seen, with the possible exception of Prince Harry and Meghan Markle's. But Harry and Meghan didn't invite me to theirs; Randall and Felicity did. They invited more than 800 people to the event, which was held at the Trump (yeah, that Trump) Taj Mahal in Atlantic City. The price tag, according to those in the know at the time, was $800,000. Today, something similar probably would cost about four times that much.

I remember driving down the Atlantic City Expressway that day dressed in a tux and complaining my ass off to Kay about going. I had a lot of other things I needed to be doing that day. Then we got there and I didn't complain anymore.

Because I spent so much time in the locker room and playing racquetball with the players, Randall and I had become pretty good friends. Kay and I were part of a slightly smaller group that was invited to the ceremony as well as the reception. When we first walked into the ceremony, I felt kind of out of place. I noticed four ushers in the back. Two of them I knew—they were teammates of Randall's—and the other two I didn't recognize.

The music started, and I was immediately enthralled. I love showbiz, and Randall was the essence of showbiz. Randall and I would occasionally talk about the entertainment world in our conversations in the locker room. Some of the pre-ceremony entertainment that day included Johnny Gill from the popular R&B group New Edition and Margaret Bell, a Christian R&B singer who was married to Keith Byars. In fact, Margaret and Johnny performed an unbelievable duet, singing the famous Simon and Garfunkel song "Bridge Over Troubled Water." It was incredible. As much as I love the Eagles Pep Band, that duet was much better than "Fly, Eagles, Fly."

There were 26 people in the wedding party! Most of the groomsmen were players on the team. All of them did a choreographed strut down the aisle. Boy, was I into that wedding. Suddenly Randall entered and walked to the front of the room, turned around, and simply pointed. *Bang*, the lights went out and two spotlights came on. Remember those two ushers in the back who I didn't recognize? Well, they broke into a dance. Turned out they were part of Felicity's dance troupe.

They were fantastic, as you can imagine. They finished their performance on a platform with sliding-glass doors. The area inside the doors was filled with smoke or steam. Out of that smoke or steam walked the bride. What an entrance! It was something I'll never forget. The reception wasn't too shabby either. They had two huge ice sculptures; one was of a football player and the other was of a ballet dancer. It was pretty impressive.

Randall spent 11 seasons with the Eagles. He succeeded in spite of Buddy Ryan, not because of him. With a better coach, he might be in the Hall of Fame today. Ryan only cared about the defensive side of the ball. His idea of an offensive game plan was to let Randall run around and make five or six big plays with his legs. He actually said that.

Randall never became as complete a quarterback as he could have become. I mean, this guy had Hall of Fame talent. He used to wear a T-shirt that said "Let me be me." He was content to ad-lib and rely on his incredible skills rather than learn the intricacies of the quarterback position. Ryan was content with that as well and never pressed him to stay in the pocket and go through his progressions or better understand what defenses were doing against him.

Randall's career with the Eagles ended in an unfortunate way. In 1995 he lost his starting job to Rodney Peete a month into the season. With Peete as the starter, the Eagles finished 10–6 and made the playoffs in Ray Rhodes's first year as head coach. They rolled past the Detroit Lions 58–37 in the wild-card round as the defense intercepted six passes and Peete threw three touchdown passes.

But then they had to play the Dallas Cowboys—who had won the NFC East with a 12–4 record—in the second round. The two teams had split their two regular-season meetings, each winning in its own stadium. Because the Cowboys won the division, the third game was in Dallas. Randall had been all but forgotten after getting benched early in the season. His mind was on other things. He had pretty much decided to retire after the season; plus, Felicity was expecting their first child.

The week before the Cowboys game, Randall asked the team for permission to fly home to Las Vegas and spend a couple days with his pregnant wife, who was going to go into labor any minute. They gladly gave him the green light. The trouble was, Randall failed to take his playbook, including the team's offensive game plan, with him to Vegas. Amazingly, the team also didn't bother getting a contact number for Randall in Vegas. Well, Felicity gave birth to Randall II on January 4, three days before the Eagles' game with the Cowboys. But Randall didn't return to Philly; he stayed in Las Vegas with his wife and newborn for two more days, then flew directly to Dallas.

Randall obviously was ill-prepared for the game, which wouldn't have been a problem if Peete had stayed healthy. But he didn't; he suffered a concussion trying to run for a first down on the last play of the first quarter. Rhodes had no choice but to send in Cunningham, who not only hadn't attended practice all week but knew nothing about the game plan against the Cowboys defense. He was basically flying blind and ad-libbing on almost every play. The Cowboys defense had him for lunch.

Randall ended up completing just 11 of 26 passes for 161 yards and no touchdowns as the Eagles got hammered 30–11. The Cowboys went on to win their third Super Bowl in four years.

Randall did indeed announce his retirement after the 1995 season. He went back to Las Vegas and opened up a granite business of all things. But he missed football, and a year later, he returned to the NFL as a backup with the Minnesota Vikings.

He had one last hurrah. In his second season with the Vikings, in 1998, their starting quarterback, Brad Johnson, got hurt and Randall replaced him. With future Hall of Fame wide receivers Randy Moss and Cris Carter to throw to, the 35-year-old Cunningham just aired it out with his cannon of an arm and let them go catch the ball. He threw a career-high 34 touchdown passes and led the league in passing (106.0) and yards per attempt (8.7) as the Vikings went 15–1 and made it all the way to the NFC Championship Game, where they were narrowly beaten by the Falcons. Cunningham spent another year with the Vikings, then a year apiece as a backup with Dallas and Baltimore before retiring for good after the 2001 season.

Randall—who always was a spiritual guy—became an ordained minister and opened Remnant Ministries in Las Vegas in 2004. He and Felicity had three children: Randall II, who was a four-time All-American high jumper at USC; Vashti, who is one of the world's top female high jumpers; and Christian. Christian tragically drowned in a pool accident in 2010 when he was just two years old.

My heart broke for Randall when Christian died. There can be nothing tougher to deal with in this world than burying a child. But Randall and Felicity relied on their faith to help get them through that difficult period and seem to have come out on the other side.

Chapter 24

A Special Pair of Heroes

I've met a lot of nice people in my 50-plus years in professional football. Everybody hears about the negative stuff, but some of the best people I've ever met were professional football players and coaches. Sure, there are a few bad apples here and there, but most of them are really nice people.

Brian Westbrook and Brian Dawkins always will have a special place in my heart. Westbrook is one of the greatest running backs in Eagles history. His 9,785 rushing and receiving yards in eight seasons with the Eagles are the most in franchise history. He's third in rushing yards (5,995) and third in touchdowns (68). Westbrook's 90 receptions in 2007 were the most ever by an Eagle until Zach Ertz finally topped that in 2018 with 116 catches, which is also the most ever by an NFL tight end. During Westbrook's eight seasons with the Eagles, they made the playoffs six times, won four division titles, and made it to the NFC Championship Game three times and the Super Bowl once. In 2015 he was inducted into the team's Hall of Fame.

Dawkins was one of the most popular players in Eagles history—maybe *the* most popular. He was the straw that stirred the drink on those great Jim Johnson defenses in the early 2000s. Dawkins redefined the safety position in the NFL. He was a game changer, a difference maker. He was a fierce hitter and a tremendous playmaker with cornerback speed who could cover any receiver on the field. He is the only defensive player

Sharing a moment at the Linc with former Eagles RB Brian Westbrook and former Eagles offensive tackle Tra Thomas. That's my grandson R.J. on the right.

in league history at any position with more than 25 interceptions, sacks, and forced fumbles. In 2018, in just his second year of eligibility, Dawk was inducted into the Pro Football Hall of Fame.

But none of that comprises why those two guys always will have a special place in my heart. As I mentioned earlier, I have 22 grandchildren. One of them, Leo III, was diagnosed with Hodgkin's lymphoma about 12 years ago, when he was in sixth grade. The news hit me like a bus. I was scared to death, and so were his parents. The survival rate for Hodgkin's today is about 86 percent if it's diagnosed early, but 12 years ago, the number was considerably lower.

Leo spent a lot of time early on after he was diagnosed at the Children's Hospital of Philadelphia (CHOP). It became his second home. Not surprisingly, Leo was a big fan of the Eagles, particularly the two Brians.

As it happened, they were at CHOP for some sort of a scheduled appearance one day when Leo was there. Rich Burg, who was a member of our public relations staff at the time and who now is an assistant athletic director at Temple University, was at the hospital with them and found out Leo was there. He mentioned it to the two Brians as they were walking out. Well, they immediately did an about-face and went up to Leo's room to say hello. He was having a procedure done, but when he returned to his room, there were his two heroes standing there to greet him. You can just imagine the look on his face. Christmas came early. I just put my arms around both of them and said, "I will never, ever forget you." To this day, I tear up when I think about those two beautiful people and the smile they put on a scared child's face that day.

Me and Dawk in 2007.

That season, Leo happened to be at an Eagles game with his dad. I was on the field and talking to Dawk and pointed to where Leo and his dad were sitting in the lower level. Dawk ran over to where they were and greeted them and gave Leo his gloves. You can only imagine what that meant to an 11-year-old kid who was going through what he was going through. It definitely lifted his spirits.

Cancer is a tough thing to deal with, especially when you're that young. If the cancer doesn't kill you, the treatment—the chemo and the radiation—will. Leo lost all of his hair and was down to 47 pounds at one point. But thank the Lord, he eventually went into remission and is doing great. He's a healthy, terrific 23-year-old man now.

Chapter 25

Hey, Mister, Can I Have Your Shirt?

The first time I met Chad Lewis was in the ticket lobby at Veterans Stadium in 1997. Chad, a tight end out of BYU, had signed with the Eagles as an undrafted free agent that spring and made the team as a backup. He was standing in the lobby waiting to pick up tickets for a game. It was casual Friday and I was wearing a Hawaiian shirt. He saw me and said, "Hey, mister, I like your shirt." I looked at him curiously and said thanks. Then he said, "Can I have it?"

Now, Chad's a pretty big guy. He's 6'6" and something like 255 pounds. I'm 5'9". I looked at him and laughed. There were other people around, so I knew he wasn't going to come over and rip it off my scrawny back. "No, you can't have it," I said. He countered by saying, "Suppose I score a touchdown on Sunday. Will you give it to me then?" We were playing the Dallas Cowboys on national television that week. I said, "You still can't have it."

At that point, I didn't even know his name. But he wouldn't quit. He said, "OK, how about if I score the winning touchdown on Sunday? Will you give it to me then?" I finally relented. I said, "Sure. You got it, big guy. Score the winning touchdown, and I'll give you the shirt." Then I went back to my office and promptly forgot about the whole episode.

171

Well, you can probably figure out what happened next. That Sunday, with about three minutes left in the game, we were trailing the Cowboys 12–6. Rodney Peete was our quarterback, and he engineered a drive down the field. With about 30 seconds left in the game, we had the ball at the Dallas 8-yard line. At that point, our tight ends coach, Ted Williams, sent Chad into the game. It was the one and only time he took an offensive snap the whole game. Well, Peete faked a handoff to the running back, the defensive back got faked out of his jock and fell down, and Chad was standing there wide open in the end zone. Rodney threw the ball to him and Chad caught it to win the game 13–12. Chad only had 12 catches that season but four of them were for touchdowns, including that one.

Naturally, after the game, the reporters swarmed around Chad's locker to get his thoughts on scoring the game-winning touchdown. He said, "Right before the ball was snapped, I was thinking about getting that guy's shirt up in the ticket office." They all gave him a mystified "What the hell is he talking about?" look, but they eventually figured it out and came up to me later for a comment. One of them said, "I hear you bet your shirt on the game." I told him I don't bet. I think I called it a "casual arrangement."

The next day, Chad came prancing into my office and asked for the shirt. I knew he'd follow through, so I had brought it with me. We went down to the locker room and I handed it to him in front of a crowd of reporters. Chad even talked about the shirt in his 2009 memoir, *Surround Yourself with Greatness.*

Chad and I became good friends after that. He's one of the finest gentlemen I've ever met. He spent nine years in the NFL. He caught 69 passes for the Eagles in 2000 when they made the playoffs for the first time under Andy Reid, and he caught six touchdown passes the next year when they again made the playoffs. Andy, who also went to BYU—and, like Lewis, was a Mormon—loved the hell out of Chad. Chad was a hard guy not to like.

In the 2004 NFC Championship Game, Chad caught the game-clinching touchdown pass against Atlanta that sent the Eagles to their first Super Bowl in 24 years. Unfortunately, he suffered a foot injury on the play, which kept him out of the Super Bowl loss to the Patriots. I know that not being able to play in Super Bowl XXXIX was one of the great disappointments of his career.

A few years back, after he wrote his book, he was in town for a bunch of book signings. He called me and asked me to accompany him. I was honored. There I was, sitting next to him at Barnes & Noble and Borders and the Stadium Club as people stood in line to have him autograph their books.

A boy came up with a book and told Chad he liked soccer more than football. Chad signed his book and said, "Well, good luck in your soccer career." He wouldn't hand him back the book, though. He gave it to me, and I signed it "Leo Carlin, page 186." That was the page that had the story about the Hawaiian shirt bet.

Chad and I keep in touch, but I haven't asked him about the shirt lately. Knowing him, he probably still has it. Or maybe he uses it as a dust rag now.

Chapter 26

Don't Come Any Closer, Asshole

In 1970 we were a bad team; we won only three games that season. We had two cornerbacks by the names of Richard Harvey and Ed Hayes. Richard and Ed weren't very good, at least from an NFL perspective. I don't think either one of them lasted more than a year or two in the league. That year, they seemed to get blamed for every touchdown the defense gave up.

We hadn't moved out of Franklin Field yet, so our offices still were in the old Bulletin Building at 30th and Market. That's where people would come to buy their tickets. One morning, one of the guys who was helping us with ticket sales came running into my office in a panic. "Leo! Leo!" he shouted. "We just got robbed!" I looked outside and saw a couple guys in a hurry getting ready to run across Market St. I asked our guy, "Is that them?" He said it was.

I was furious and did something that wasn't terribly smart: I ran after them. I took off across Market and down 32nd or 33rd St. They were both young, well-built kids, and pretty damn fast. But I was in good shape back then and actually was gaining on them. At some point it dawned on them that I was chasing after them. That's when they stopped and turned around. No, they weren't surrendering to me. One of them pulled

175

Me in my office at 30th & Market in the late '60s, when I still was young and foolish.

out a gun and pointed it at me. "Don't come any closer, asshole," he said. I suddenly got smart and stopped. Thankfully, the guy didn't pull the trigger, or these memoirs would be much, much shorter. He tucked the gun back in his coat and they ran away.

Somebody claimed to have seen them remove a manhole cover and head into the city's sewer system. I didn't know if that was true or not. I do know they never were caught, though we're not talking about the Great Train Robbery here. As it turned out, they only got away with about $200. To think I risked my life for $200 that wasn't even mine.

I realized pretty quickly that chasing after them was stupid, but Leonard Tose reiterated that fact to me the next day. Leonard couldn't have cared less about losing $200, which wasn't surprising given the fact that we often couldn't get him to understand the significance of losing $2 million.

The robbery story—and the story about me giving chase—was in all the papers the next day. I was sitting at my desk reading one of the accounts when one of our assistant coaches, Charlie Gauer, walked in. Charlie played for the Eagles in the mid-1940s and coached the wide receivers and tight ends at the time. Charlie was a member of the Steagles in 1943—a combination of the Eagles and Pittsburgh Steelers, who had to merge their rosters that year after losing so many players to military service during World War II.

Charlie was one of the funniest guys I've ever known—very sarcastic. The first words out of his mouth when he walked in were, "Hello, stupid." As I recall, the word "jackass" also was mentioned. He asked me if they had caught the guys. When I told him they hadn't, he said, "Well, tell the cops to stop looking. I know who they are." I was confused. "What the hell are you talking about?" I asked. He said, "Well, if you were gaining on them, then it had to have been Hayes and Harvey."

Chapter 27

Taking Care of Business

Back in the 1960s and '70s, I served as the Eagles' business manager as well as the ticket manager. One of the myriad responsibilities I had as business manager was handing out the paychecks to players, including at training camp.

In the summer of 1974, the players had staged a 41-day strike, from July 1 (training camps opened earlier back then) through August 10. It was the middle of August, the strike was over, and I was handing out checks to the players after they returned to camp.

We had a defensive lineman on the team at the time named Will Wynn. Will was a good player. He was a seventh-round pick out of Tennessee State in 1973 who quickly became one of the team's most productive starters. Will and I were friends, but when I handed him his check that day, he took it and angrily threw it at me. The check was prorated because of the strike. It wasn't nearly as much as Will thought it was going to be.

If you think I was furious when I went chasing after those two guys who robbed the ticket office back in 1970, that was nothing compared to how angry I was when Will hurled his check at me. I said something to him and told him he couldn't treat me like that. We then got into a screaming match. There were about a hundred guys standing around watching the two of us holler at each other—me a 5'9", 150-pound business manager/ticket manager and him a 6'4", 250-pound NFL defensive lineman. Can you say major mismatch?

We finally stopped yelling and I walked over to the meeting area where everybody else was. It was like the parting of the Red Sea as all of the players stepped aside as this little guy walked through. At that point, I realized how hysterical the whole thing was and started to laugh.

Will passed away of heart failure in 2013. He lived in the Philly area and often came to games. Before he died, I told him I was going to put that story in my book. He laughed.

Being the team's business manager wasn't all it was cracked up to be. In 1969, when the team still held training camp at Albright College in Reading, we acquired a couple of offensive linemen in a trade with the Rams—Don Chuy and Joe Carollo. Don was a fun-loving guy who often could be seen jumping into a pool at Albright with nothing on but his cowboy boots. Today that would get you jail time for public exposure, but back then it was just considered one of those wacky things football players did.

After we traded for the two of them, both had borrowed $15,000 from the team. When it came time to pay the loan back, Don had no interest in doing so. My good friend Pete Retzlaff was the team's general manager at the time. He told me to confront Chuy and ask him for the money, and if he refused, try to get him to hit me. Seriously, Pete really said that, and I actually tried it. I called Don a few choice names and said, "You're one of the first players I ever helped get a loan from this team, and you're going to be the last." Chuy didn't bite. He looked at me calmly and said, "I guess so." So much for my powers of intimidation. We ended up suing him and going to court, and I had to testify. I still don't remember if we got the money from him or not.

I saw Chuy some years later and he told me how unbalanced he was back then, and that he had even contemplated killing himself at one point. He said he took his dog and a rifle into the woods but didn't follow through. Don lived a long life and died of natural causes in 2014 at his home in Myrtle Beach, South Carolina.

Around the same time that Will Wynn and I had our run-in, we had another defensive end on the team by the name of Joe "Turkey" Jones. Back then, there used to be a "holdback" rule, where the team hung on to 25 percent of a player's salary until after the last game of the season, kind of like a security deposit on an apartment. Can you imagine teams getting away with that today? Well, Turkey spent much of his season and a half with the Eagles living at the Holiday Inn at 10th and Packer, next to the stadium. He had partied so much during his stay there his first season with the team that the entire holdback check was given to the hotel for all the bills he had accumulated and not paid. Thankfully, he didn't get upset when I gave him the bad news.

Chapter 28

The Man Who KO'd Csonka

I was in my early twenties when I first started working for the Eagles, which meant I was about the same age as many of the players. In those early years, I became friends with quite a few of them and would occasionally have a drink or go out to dinner with them. When Jerry Wolman and Ed Snyder added business manager to my title in 1965, I started traveling with the team.

One player I became particularly close with was a linebacker by the name of Dave Lloyd. We were really nothing alike. He was a smart player with a strong personality. I was Richie Cunningham. But surprisingly, we got along. On road trips, he wouldn't let anybody but me sit next to him on the plane or bus.

Dave didn't mind breaking an occasional team rule now and then. One time we were in Los Angeles for a game against the Rams. I bumped into Dave in the hotel lobby after he came out of the team's defensive meeting and he suggested we go somewhere and get a drink. The defensive coordinator at the time was really strict, and I was scared to death he was going to get caught. But Dave was a seasoned veteran and had his spots in every town that he knew weren't frequented by the coaches or team personnel. Thankfully, we made it back for curfew.

After Leonard Tose bought the team in the spring of 1969 and fired Joe Kuharich, he hired Jerry Williams as his new head coach. Jerry had played for the Eagles in the mid-1950s and was an assistant with the team from 1957 to 1963. He was coaching in Canada when Leonard hired him. Anyway, Jerry wasn't a big fan of Dave's. Lloyd, who had just turned 33, was a 10-year NFL veteran who had been with the Eagles for six seasons. Before training camp opened in 1969, Williams went to him and bluntly informed him that he didn't think he could play anymore and that he was going to cut him as soon as he got the chance.

Dave never reported to training camp in very good shape. The summer of 1969 was no exception. After running his first 40-yard sprint on the first day of camp, he promptly threw up. Williams and his defensive assistants were on a mission that summer to run Lloyd out of camp. They were constantly on him, telling him he sucked and that he should start thinking about a career after football. But that just ignited the competitive fire in Dave. He slowly played himself into shape. He had been a starter his entire career. But Williams basically had dropped him to the bottom of the depth chart.

In those days, teams played six preseason games. Our last preseason opponent that summer was the Miami Dolphins. Lloyd wasn't expected to play much, if at all, in that game, but injuries had left the team with almost no healthy linebackers. With no other options, they sent in Dave.

The thing about Dave was, while age might've robbed him of some of his physical tools, he was an incredibly smart player who could anticipate what the offense was going to do. On a third-and-15 play, the Dolphins ran a draw play. Dave read the play, came up, and met the runner in the hole. The runner was Larry Csonka, a bruising rusher who would go on to help the Dolphins win two Super Bowl championships and later was inducted into the Pro Football Hall of Fame. Well, Dave hit Csonka and knocked the SOB out. I'm talking la-la land. They had to carry Larry off the field.

After that play, Dave ran off the field, went right up to Williams, got in his face, and told him to stick all of his over-the-hill bullshit up his rectum. Not only did Lloyd not get cut that season, he ended up making the Pro Bowl.

Chapter 29
No Freedom, No Football

During my time with the Eagles, there were several work stoppages. There was a 12-day strike before the start of the 1968 season that resulted in the formation of the NFL Players Association and the league's first collective bargaining agreement.

Then in 1974 the players went on strike for 42 days during training camp. The main issue then, as with the two strikes that followed in 1982 and 1987, was free agency. The players wanted it, and the owners treated it like the bubonic plague. The players' slogan during the '74 strike was "No freedom, no football." The owners insisted that giving the players free agency would create "anarchy." When the players finally got free agency in the early 1990s, it wasn't through a work stoppage but a lawsuit and a sympathetic judge.

During the '74 strike, the Eagles players held a disaster of a meeting at a local hotel. It was supposed to be a secret meeting to discuss whether the players should cross the picket line. Except it wasn't very secret; everybody knew about it. Leonard Tose tried to get them to take a vote with no discussion because he had certain players ready to cross. But he found out that day that he didn't have enough players ready to cross.

I remember one of our coaches, Boyd Dowler, saying after that meeting that we had just driven a wedge right down the middle of the team, and he was right. The rift between players over crossing the picket line lingered long after the strike was over and caused serious damage to team unity.

The '74 strike was doomed from the start. A month into it, a quarter of the league's players had already crossed the picket line. When peace finally was declared in August, none of the players' demands, including free agency, had been met.

The players struck for 57 days in 1982. That year, the league ended up having to eliminate much of the season and play a nine-game schedule, followed by a 16-team playoff tournament to determine the Super Bowl champion.

Five years later, in 1987, the players struck for 24 days. That one got particularly ugly because the owners signed replacement players, or "scabs" as they were called by the striking players and their union supporters. The owners played three weeks' worth of games that season with replacement players. Remember Guido Merkens? Topper Clemons? George Cumby? Kelly Kirchbaum? As mentioned, Buddy Ryan—who was the Eagles' coach then—hated the whole idea of replacement games. He made fun of his replacement players and basically turned over the coaching to his assistants. That worked out really well; the Eagles lost all three replacement games and finished 7–8.

That 1987 strike was an ugly mess. In Philly, the testosterone started to flow right away, and other unions quickly got involved. And many of the players weren't experienced enough in labor matters to keep them under control. At the first replacement game, we had dozens of trucks driving around the stadium trying to block people from getting inside. The team's player representative, Yale-educated John Spagnola, called a meeting at FDR Park across the street from the stadium, but the leaders of other unions in the city took over the meeting.

I still remember one of the union leaders going up to John, who was at least eight inches taller than the guy, and telling him, "Get out of here. We're taking over now." And there was nothing John could do about it. Sure, he could have squashed the guy like a bug. But that would have just set off a war. It was weird to see these union people scare the hell out of our big, tough players. I mean, the players could have beaten them all to a pulp, but they were completely intimidated by them because labor fights weren't their thing.

As the strike went on, the players lost their enthusiasm for the fight. The picket lines got lighter and lighter. I remember one time going out and asking Joe Conwell, an offensive tackle who was a friend of mine, if he could give me a ride home. He didn't even have to think about it. He was thrilled to get out of there for the day.

The most recent work stoppage occurred in 2011. That one actually wasn't a strike but a lockout by the owners. It lasted from March until August. With the exception of the draft, all off-season activity was shut down. Free agency, which usually starts in March, was condensed to a small period in August after the players and owners agreed to a new 10-year collective bargaining agreement.

Chapter 30
Just Call Me Coach

Like me, Burt Grossman was a Philly kid. He played his high school ball at Archbishop Carroll, earned a scholarship to Pitt, and ended up being the eighth overall pick in the 1989 draft by the San Diego Chargers. Grossman, a defensive end, only played six seasons in the NFL before a neck injury ended his career. He played five with the Chargers before being traded to his hometown team, the Eagles, in 1994 for what turned out to be his last season in professional football.

Burt didn't get to play a long time, but he was productive when he did play. He had 45 sacks in his five seasons with the Chargers. I can take some credit for his success because I was his eighth-grade coach. I kid. I really was Burt's eighth-grade coach, but I didn't do anything that helped him become a successful NFL player. Burt, who would top out at 6'4" and 275 pounds, already was a big kid the year I coached him. His size had a lot more to do with his success that year than anything I taught him. In fact, to give you an idea of what a great judge of football flesh I was, I didn't think Burt was going to amount to much as a player because he didn't like to hustle as a young kid. Next thing I knew, he was an all–Catholic League player at Carroll and an All-American at Pitt and one of the top picks in the 1989 draft.

During the one season Burt played for the Eagles, he would often come into the ticket office and ask the girls working the counter if "Uncle

191

Leo" was back there, because he knew he could always get more tickets out of me than he could from the girls. He and I had a lot of fun during the season he played for us. Burt was a great guy.

Four of the seven players taken ahead of Burt in the '89 draft—Troy Aikman, Barry Sanders, the late Derrick Thomas, and Deion Sanders—are in the Pro Football Hall of Fame. The other three taken ahead of him were offensive tackle Tony Mandarich (second pick, by the Packers), linebacker Broderick Thomas (sixth pick, by the Bucs), and running back Tim Worley (seventh pick, by the Steelers).

Mandarich was one of the all-time draft busts. He was a product of steroids who lasted only three years with the Packers before they got rid of him. Addicted to both drugs and alcohol, Mandarich—with help from his parents—got sober and got his life together and eventually gave football one more try. He signed with the Indianapolis Colts four

Sharing a laugh with Tom Brookshier. He played for the Eagles from 1953 to 1961 and later joined Pat Summerall on CBS's top NFL broadcast team.

years after the Packers cut him and started 32 games in three seasons for them. Broderick Thomas had a solid career. He played nine years in the league and made 96 starts. Worley rushed for 770 yards as a rookie with the Steelers then petered out. He stuck around five more years but only rushed for 1,022 more yards in his last five seasons.

Burt wasn't a Hall of Fame–caliber player, but he would have had a long, productive career if he had been able to stay healthy, which I guess you can say about a lot of guys who pass through the NFL.

Burt was very outspoken; he didn't know how to hold his tongue. He had an opinion on everything. I remember early in his career with San Diego, he made the cover of *Sports Illustrated*. His picture was alongside the tagline, "Big Mouth." The story chronicled his outspoken personality. He was a productive player for the Chargers, but his outspokenness could rub the people he worked for the wrong way. After he missed six games in 1993 with a bunch of nagging injuries and his sack total dropped from 8 the year before to just 4.5, Chargers GM Bobby Beathard traded him to the Eagles for a sixth-round pick.

I'm not sure what happened with him in Philly. He got there just after Jeffrey Lurie had bought the team from Norman Braman. Rich Kotite was on his way out as the head coach. Burt had played on the left side in San Diego but was moved to the right side by Eagles defensive coordinator Bud Carson before the start of the 1994 season. He just wasn't the same player on the right side. His playing time and productivity both dropped. The '94 season was the one where the Eagles got off to a 7–2 start, then went into a 0–7 free-fall.

Burt got his bachelor's degree in sociology and a master's in education and public policy. He became the codirector of a program for at-risk youth at San Diego's Hoover High School and made such an impact at the inner-city school that he was named the NFL's Teacher of the Year back in 2011. Burt also got into coaching. He coached at Hoover and for the last two years has been the head coach of the San Diego Strike Force of the Indoor Football League.

Chapter 31
Death and Football

It's funny how particular moments become etched in your mind forever, such as the 6:00 AM phone call I got from Jim Solano five days before Christmas in 1976. Jimmy was a longtime friend. He also was an agent who represented dozens of Eagles players over the years, including one of our defensive linemen back then, Blenda Gay. I picked up the phone and Jimmy said, "Leo, Blenda Gay's wife killed him last night."

We had signed Blenda the year before. He had been cut by both the Raiders and Chargers and was playing in a semipro league somewhere. He ended up starting eight games for us in 1975 and 13 in '76, which was Dick Vermeil's first season as the team's head coach.

Blenda's wife's name was Roxanne. She cut his throat in the middle of the night while he was sleeping. She said she did it in self-defense because she was a longtime victim of physical and verbal abuse by her husband. That was a different time; domestic abuse wasn't treated with the same seriousness that it is now. The case became a cause célèbre for the feminist movement back then. Gloria Steinem and *Ms.* magazine raised money for Roxanne's defense.

Police confirmed that Roxanne had made nearly two dozen 9-1-1 calls to police about her husband. But Blenda had never been jailed or arrested. I don't know whether it is true or not, but *Ms.* magazine reported that when the police would show up after she'd call them about her husband beating her, they would talk football with Blenda and then leave. Nevertheless, a panel of psychiatrists claimed Roxanne had fabricated the stories of abuse by her husband. She was diagnosed with schizophrenia and put in a psychiatric hospital. The charges against her were dropped, and she spent about three years in the hospital before being released.

Blenda's murder was a big story in Philadelphia back then, and it sent shock waves through the organization. But life went on. Just as it had five years earlier when Chuck Hughes became the first—and so far only—player in league history to die during a game.

Chuck, who was one of 16 children, was a wide receiver out of Texas Western who the Eagles selected in the fourth round of the 1967 draft. I thought Chuck, who once caught 17 passes in a game in college, had a chance to be a pretty good player for us. I still remember a long catch he made in a preseason game as a rookie. But we had some pretty good wide receivers back then, including Ben Hawkins and Harold Jackson and Fred Hill and Gary Ballman. Chuck was with us for three seasons but caught only six passes. In 1970 we traded him to the Detroit Lions.

He started nine games for the Lions in 1970 but caught only eight passes. A year later he was back on the bench, behind their three top receivers: Ron Jessie, Earl McCullough, and Larry Walton. He played in just two of the Lions' first five games in 1971 and didn't get into the sixth game until there were fewer than two minutes left, following an injury to Walton. With the Lions trailing by five, Hughes caught a 32-yard pass from quarterback Greg Landry. It was his first catch of the year, and it would be the last catch of his life.

Three plays later, on third-and-10, Hughes lined up on the right side. The cornerback who was covering him on that play would later say his eyes "looked kind of strange." Hughes ran a down-and-in route. The ball was thrown to the Lions' tight end, Charlie Sanders, on the play.

As Hughes jogged back to the huddle, he suddenly clutched his chest and collapsed on the 20-yard line. Doctors tried to revive him but were unsuccessful. An autopsy later determined that he died of acute coronary thrombosis brought on by premature hardening of the arteries.

It was later reported that Chuck had complained of chest pain to the Lions' medical staff earlier in the season, but they couldn't find anything and cleared him to play. His widow ended up suing the Lions, the team doctors, and the hospital. The suit was settled out of court.

Chuck's funeral was in San Antonio. To his credit, even though Chuck no longer was with the Eagles, Leonard Tose rented a Lear jet and several of us from the organization flew down there for the service. We flew back the same day. What a difficult scene that was to watch, especially considering Chuck had a two-year-old son.

Chapter 32

Some People I've Met Along the Way

I have precious few regrets about the 50-plus years I spent in professional football. It truly was an incredible journey. There's not much I would change. How many other people can say they zip-lined across Lincoln Financial Field or rappelled from the top of a stadium? I've done both.

I zip-lined two or three times. It was the most incredible feeling in the world. That first step, you don't know what's going to happen. Then the next second, you're floating through the air and feel fantastic. I loved it. There I was, with 7 kids and 22 grandchildren, and I was zip-lining over an NFL stadium. Hysterical. Everybody knew about it. Well, almost everybody. I didn't tell Kay until after I did it the first time. When I explained it to her, she nearly had a heart attack. She wasn't happy with me. It was similar to the time I came home from rough-touch football with a broken jaw.

I've had the opportunity to get to know and become friends with a lot of people in this game during my many years in football, the famous and the not so famous. Players. Coaches. Front-office executives. Owners. Trainers. Doctors. Equipment people. Mascots. Secretaries. Janitors. The list goes on and on. Here are my reflections on just a few of them:

Standing in front of a mural of Eagles Pro Bowlers at the team's NovaCare training facility.

George McCaskey is one of my favorite people in the NFL. George has been the chairman of the Chicago Bears since 2011, when he took over for his brother Michael, who retired. He was named after his grandfather George Halas, who founded the Bears. George McCaskey was an assistant state's attorney in Illinois and also worked in broadcasting briefly before joining the family business in 1991 and becoming the Bears' ticket manager.

I once was given a tremendous compliment by George's late father, Ed McCaskey, when he ran the Bears. After George became the Bears' ticket director, his father told him that if he had any problems in that position, he should call the ticket guy in Philadelphia, meaning me. "He'll be able to take care of it for you," Ed told his son. George did call me, and that began a long friendship that still exists today.

One of my very best friends in the NFL back in the late 1960s and early '70s was wide receiver Ben Hawkins. Ben, who remained a close friend until he passed away in 2017. He was a third-round pick of the Eagles in 1966 and played eight seasons for them.

The Eagles weren't very good when Ben played for them. They had only one winning season during his eight years with the team. That was his rookie year, when they went 9–5 under Joe Kuharich. That said, Ben was a very good player. He led the league in receiving yards in 1967 and also had 10 touchdown catches that year. He averaged 18.3 yards per catch during his career, which is nearly a yard better than DeSean Jackson. He's tied with Hall of Famer James Lofton at 23rd all-time in the NFL for yards per catch.

Ben was one of the best athletes I've ever seen. I remember one time we were practicing at Franklin Field. He came out of the locker room in full equipment. Franklin Field, which is on the campus of the University of Pennsylvania, also has a track, where, among other things, they run the famous Penn Relays every year. Anyway, some of the college kids were over on the track doing the high hurdles. Ben went over and ran the high hurdles in full equipment.

Ben was the only Eagles player I know who was responsible for an NFL rule change. He was famous for never buckling his chinstrap; he played with it dangling down. Finally the league, worried somebody was going to get his neck broken doing that, instituted a rule forcing players to have their chinstraps buckled during plays. Ben wasn't happy with the rule.

Right up until he died, Ben would occasionally come to games. It was strange to see such a great player from the past, a guy who is in the team's Hall of Fame, sit there in the crowd and go unrecognized by most of the people around him. Fame is indeed fleeting.

I've known Harold Carmichael since his playing days. He's one of the best wide receivers in franchise history. At 6'8" and 225 pounds, he was a huge target with an enormous catch radius. He played for the Eagles

My friend Harold Carmichael, who is a member of the Pro Football Hall of Fame class of 2020.

from 1971 through 1983. From 1973 to 1983, he led all NFL receivers in catches, receiving yards, and touchdowns. He was named to the NFL's All-Decade Team of the 1970s. In January 2020, at the age of 70, Harold finally was selected to the Pro Football Hall of Fame. Talk about a long-overdue honor.

Harold is a wonderful man. In 1980 he not only helped Dick Vermeil's Eagles get to the Super Bowl but also was named the NFL Man of the Year for all his charitable work with groups such as Eagles Fly for Leukemia, the United Way, and the Boy Scouts of America. Harold is the type of friend who would do anything for you.

In 1998, 14 years after he retired and four years after Jeffrey Lurie bought the team, the Eagles brought Harold back to the organization and made him their director of player and community relations. He served in that role for 17 years, retiring the same year I did, in 2015. He continues to serve as a team ambassador.

Harold is one of 10 "senior" players (players who haven't played in at least 30 years) who are being inducted into Canton this summer as part of the Hall's special centennial class of 2020. When it was announced Harold had made the Hall of Fame, the Eagles had a special celebration for him at the NovaCare Complex. I had the honor of being there for it.

Harold found out he was being inducted into the Hall of Fame two days before the announcement was actually made. The NFL Network wanted to bring a few of the inductees, including Harold, out to Los Angeles to appear on their morning show, *Good Morning Football*, as soon as the announcement was made, so they gave him advance warning. Harold said he was watching one of his favorite TV shows, *The Rifleman*, when he got a call from David Baker, who is the president of the Pro Football Hall of Fame.

"First thing I thought, there are these radio stations that will punk you," Harold said. "They have somebody pretend to be somebody you know. When he told me I had made the Hall of Fame, that's what was going through my mind: *Is somebody trying to punk me here?* But he finally convinced me it was legit."

Baker called Harold on a Monday afternoon, and the official announcement wasn't going to be made until that Wednesday morning. Baker asked Harold not to tell anybody but his wife, B (short for Beatrice), that he had made it. For the better part of 40 hours, the only people who knew he had made the Hall of Fame were him, B, and Chuck Connors. He didn't even tell his son because he was afraid he would tell their granddaughter, who might spill the beans on social media.

He also had to keep it from Vermeil. Harold and his former coach are very close. Dick also was a finalist for the Hall of Fame this year but lost out in the coaching category to Bill Cowher and Jimmy Johnson.

The night before the official announcements, Harold spent three hours at a dinner with Dick and more than 160 other people. "I sat with him and couldn't say anything," Harold said. "It killed me. It was very tough. I told him later how disappointed I was that he didn't get in. He's been an inspiration to me for years. I love him. It would've been great for the two of us to have gone in together."

One of the most fun-loving players I've ever been around was defensive tackle Mike Golic, who played on those great Buddy Ryan–coached Eagles defensive lines with Reggie White, Jerome Brown, Clyde Simmons, and Mike Pitts in the late 1980s and early '90s. Mike would be in my office all the time, joking about his wife and family. We would exchange stories about our families. I'd usually come out on top since I had seven kids.

The last contract he signed with the team was a one-year deal. He came into my office with the contract in his hands, patted his stomach, and said, "Boy, I faked them out one more time." The truth is Golic didn't fake anybody out; he earned every penny he made in the NFL. He was a good, solid player. But that's the way he was: very self-deprecating. He never took himself too seriously. He was and is a terrific, fun guy whose personality and sense of humor have helped him carve out a very successful career in broadcasting.

Sam Baker was a kicker and punter with the Eagles in the 1960s. He spent the last six years of a 15-year career with us. We got Sam from the Cowboys. The word was that Tom Landry couldn't wait to get rid of him; he wasn't Tom's cup of tea. When Landry used to give one of his speeches to his players about the "Cowboy Way," Sam would start humming a song, which, as you might imagine, pissed Tom off to no end.

Sam was the team clown; he didn't take a lot of things seriously. Curfew meant nothing to him. I remember when we played the Baltimore Colts one year in the Playoff Bowl in Miami, Sam and his wife would meet us in the bar at 3:00 AM. Joe Kuharich asked him if he was getting his mail there. For those who don't remember the Playoff Bowl, it was a meaningless consolation game that was played from 1960 through 1969 between the second-place teams in the NFL's two divisions. If the game had meant anything, I don't think Kuharich would have been so understanding about Sam being in that bar at 3:00 AM.

Kevin Reilly was a seventh-round pick of the Dolphins out of Villanova but ended up with the Eagles and was the team's special teams captain in 1973 and 1974. In 1976 he was diagnosed with cancer and ended up having to have his left arm amputated. But Kevin didn't let it hold him back; he learned how to function with one arm better than most people do with two. He learned how to tie a necktie with one arm, he learned how to play golf with one arm, and he ran half marathons.

He had a 30-year career with Xerox and later got into broadcasting. He has cohosted the Eagles' pre- and postgame shows and is a color analyst for his alma mater's football games. He does motivational speaking, and he counseled victims of the Boston Marathon bombing. He's a truly inspirational person who I am honored to call a friend.

Stan Walters was our starting left tackle for nearly a decade in the 1970s and '80s. He went to two Pro Bowls and was a three-time All-Pro. He's in the Eagles Hall of Fame. Stan, who served as the team's radio color analyst for more than a decade after he retired, is one of the most intelligent people I've ever met. Notice I said *people* not *players*. Stan can discuss anything with you. We've been friends since his playing days.

Stan's wife, Kathy, was the executive vice president of the consumer products group for Georgia-Pacific. They've lived in Boston and London and Atlanta. I've run into him at a few social functions in recent years.

Another really smart guy was John Bunting, who played linebacker for both the Eagles and the USFL's Stars. John and I became racquetball buddies when he was with the Eagles. Even though he beat me pretty regularly, we became good friends. John was one of the defensive leaders of the Eagles' 1980 Super Bowl team. He also was the team's player rep during the 1982 strike. When Leonard got rid of him after the '82 season, partly because of his union activities, he signed with the Stars and was a big part of their two championships.

I've known Joe Conwell since he was a boy. He used to play in the same schoolyard as our kids when they were young. Our boys all went to St. Joe's Prep. Joe went to Lower Merion and earned a scholarship to the University of North Carolina. Joe, an offensive tackle, ended up playing two years in the USFL for the Stars. He played on both of their league championship teams then signed with the Eagles after the USFL went belly-up. He started 22 games for them in 1986–87.

Mike Evans was a center for the Eagles for six seasons, from 1968 to 1973. We became friends. He was a very self-deprecating guy. I remember when he was a rookie, he was walking out of the locker room and a kid said, "Hey, can I have your autograph?" Mike looked at him and said, "Well, I'm not going to be very good. Camp's not going very well for me, so I'm not sure you really want my autograph." The kid replied, "Ah, I'll take it anyway. If you get cut, I can always throw it away."

John Spagnola, a tight end for the Eagles from 1979 to 1987, was a Yale guy. You don't see many Ivy League players in the NFL. When John came to work, it was like he was the chairman of the board. He could speak and act that way too. He always carried himself with great dignity and was a terrific player too. He caught 60-plus passes in back-to-back years in the mid-1980s when 60-plus catches was a lot, especially for a tight end. Even though John was a very good player, I got the sense Buddy Ryan never was a big fan of his. I think he was threatened by John's intelligence. John didn't buy his bullshit.

John also was the Eagles' player rep during that ugly 1987 strike with the replacement players. That, coincidentally or not, ended up being his last year with the Eagles. John remains a good friend. On the few occasions I get to talk to him now, it's very enjoyable.

Chuck Bednarik was one of the greatest players in Eagles history. I don't need to go into all of his incredible accomplishments; they're well-documented. For better or worse, Bednarik was a very outspoken person. He said what was on his mind. Asked once about Deion Sanders playing both offense and defense, Bednarik, the last of the league's 60-minute men, said that Deion couldn't hold his jock strap. He probably should have given a more diplomatic answer, even if he didn't mean it. But that was Chuck. He became very resentful of the players who followed him in the NFL, particularly when salaries started to skyrocket. The most money Chuck ever made in a single season during his spectacular career was $27,000.

Chuck's relationship with the Eagles after he retired wasn't always the best, particularly after Jeffrey Lurie bought the team in the mid-1990s. Chuck didn't think Jeffrey, a born-and-bred New Englander, paid enough homage to the Eagles' past. When Chuck's autobiography was published in 1996, two years after Lurie bought the team, Bednarik wanted Jeffrey to buy 100 copies of the book at $15 apiece and give them to his players. Lurie couldn't do it because NFL salary cap rules prohibit teams from giving gifts to players. The Eagles tried to explain that to Chuck, but it went in one ear and out the other. He took it personally and publicly criticized Lurie, saying the $1,500 for the 100 books would've been "tip money" for him.

When Andy Reid was hired in 1999, he tried to fix the broken relationship between the Eagles and Bednarik. It seemed to work until 2004, when Bednarik openly rooted against the Eagles when they played the Patriots in the Super Bowl. A couple of years later, Bednarik—who died in 2015—finally made peace with Lurie and the organization and would occasionally attend games and club functions, which was nice to see.

Tim Brown was one of the best all-purpose backs in Eagles history. He was Brian Westbrook before Brian Westbrook. He could run with the ball and catch it, and he was an outstanding kick returner. Drafted by Green Bay in 1959, he joined the Eagles in 1960 and played eight years in Philly. He had 60 rushing, receiving, and return touchdowns in those eight years.

Andy Reid talking to the media at Super Bowl LIV. So glad he finally won a Super Bowl.

Timmy was a good-looking guy with a lot of talent beyond the football field. He got into acting while he still was playing football and appeared in more than three dozen movies and TV shows. He appeared in both the movie and TV versions of *M*A*S*H*. He also recorded a couple songs and even spent a year as an NFL color analyst for CBS in the early 1970s.

The Eagles weren't very good for most of the eight years Brown was in Philly. But he brought a lot of life to some of those poor teams. Joe Kuharich was his coach for four of the eight years with the Eagles. Joe didn't like Timmy much; he felt he was "too Hollywood." He thought he wasn't focused enough on football because of his other interests. But I never saw that; I saw a guy who played very well for a bunch of teams that didn't have a lot of talent around him.

Not a lot of people remember that Norm Bulaich played for the Eagles. The man known as the Human Bowling Ball spent 10 years in the league. The first three were with the Colts and the last five were with the Dolphins, but he spent 1973–74 with the Eagles. We weren't very good back then. I think we finished 5–8–1 in 1973 and 7–7 in '74. Mike McCormack was our coach back then. I remember we were getting our butts handed to us in one game. As the offense was running back out onto the field, McCormack told them they needed to start getting the ball in the end zone. To which Bulaich replied, "OK, Coach. Do you want me to win it by six points or just a field goal?" McCormack was not amused. If memory serves, I think we lost that game by 17.

In the 1970s we had a defensive tackle by the name of Bill Dunstan who trained in kung fu. He worked with Gus Hoefling, who was the Phillies' strength and flexibility instructor and had a big influence on Steve Carlton's Hall of Fame career. But Gus also worked with players in other sports, including Dunstan and quarterback Roman Gabriel.

One time, I happened to be talking to Hoefling and he showed me how to extract someone's eye. You probably won't be surprised to learn that I've never had occasion to use that technique. Not long after that, a scuffle broke out in training camp between Dunstan and another player whose name escapes me. Mike McCormack came rushing over to try and break it up. He clearly was aware that Dunstan had been working with Hoefling, because he started yelling, "No, Bill! No! Not his eye!"

In my early years with the Eagles, we had a guy who worked in sales by the name of Gene Kilroy. We used to play basketball together and became friends, though he didn't stay around very long. I kind of lost track of him after he left. Then one day a few years later, I was watching television and Muhammad Ali was on. He still was Cassius Clay back then. Anyway, he was being interviewed by somebody, and suddenly, Ali said, "I'd like to introduce you to my business manager." The camera panned to a guy in the audience, and it was none other than my buddy Gene. I almost fell out of my chair. Not long after that, Gene brought Ali to the Eagles offices to meet me. What a thrill! Ali was so subdued and quiet and gentlemanly. He stayed for about an hour, and it was fun talking to him and getting to know him.

Gene moved to Las Vegas after he left the Eagles. Kay and I went out there for a vacation once, and Gene introduced us to the great actor Tony Curtis, who starred in such movies as *Some Like It Hot*, *The Defiant Ones*, *The Outsider*, and *The Bad News Bears Go to Japan*. Hey, three out of four ain't bad.

Thanks to Mike McCormack's "future is now" roster-building approach during his three years as the Eagles' head coach from 1973 through 1975, the team did not have a single first- or second-round pick from 1974 through 1978. It also didn't have any third- or fourth-round picks in 1975, '76, and '77. Mike had traded all of those picks away for veteran players, many of whom were well past their sell-by date. That Dick Vermeil and Carl Peterson were able to overcome that lack of draft ammunition and win 11 games in 1979 and make it to the Super Bowl in 1980 was a truly amazing feat.

Before Mike started playing *Let's Make a Deal* with our draft picks, though, he had two first-round picks in the 1973 draft—the third and sixth overall selections—which he used on an offensive tackle from the

University of Texas named Jerry Sisemore and a tight end from Southern California named Charle Young. That's *Charle*, not *Charlie*.

Charle and Jerry had two very different personalities. Jerry was one of the nicest guys who ever played for the Eagles. He was a great player—a two-time Pro Bowler who started 155 games for us from 1973 until he retired in 1984—but very humble. Conversely, Charle didn't have a humble bone in his body. He was talking to reporters after we drafted him and was asked to rate himself on a scale of 1 to 10. He said he was about a 9.5. After meeting him, I was shocked he went that low.

I remember two things about Charle's first visit to Philly after he got drafted. The first is that we went out to breakfast and he ate not only his own food but mine as well. The guy had an appetite. The second is, he left his car on the street in South Philly when he came to the stadium. When he went back to his car later, it was up on blocks with all of the tires missing. What a welcome-to-Philly moment.

Charle made a big splash with the Eagles early on. He caught 55 passes for 854 yards and six touchdowns as a rookie and made first-team All-

Another day at the office, posing with Eagles mascot Swoop.

Pro. Not many rookies ever are selected All-Pro, but he was. His second year with us, he caught 63 passes for 696 yards and three touchdowns. But he peaked too soon; he played in the league for 13 seasons but never came close to matching his production in those first two seasons. Charle was with the Eagles for only 4 of those 13 years, but he ended up playing an important role in their 1980 Super Bowl appearance: he was traded to the Rams after the 1976 season for the quarterback who would lead us to the Super Bowl, Ron Jaworski.

The city of Philadelphia is blessed with two of the best mascots in existence. The Phillies have the Phanatic, and the Eagles have Swoop. Swoop's real name is Ryan Hughes. He's a great guy and does a terrific job. He's helped me with some of my highwire antics, including rappelling from the tower at Lincoln Financial Field.

Before Ryan, we had another guy who played Swoop—Jeff Alexander. As Swoop, Jeff would ride a motorcycle on the sideline and wave to the crowd. One game, he was riding his motorcycle and kind of got caught up in the action on the field and didn't see a female security guard in front of him. You can guess what happened. He accidentally hit her going pretty fast. Fortunately, the guard only suffered minor injuries, but that pretty much marked the end of Jeff's career as Swoop.

Chapter 33

The Legend of "Muss" Detty

G. E. "Moose" Detty was the Eagles' head trainer from the early 1960s until the mid-1970s. He was a very innovative guy. He came up with the idea for the neoprene sleeve that athletes wear on their arms and legs. At one point, Moose had more than 20 patents for sports medicine products. He eventually founded a company called PRO Orthopedic Devices that now is run by his son. Moose, who passed away in 2003, was inducted into the National Athletic Trainers' Association Hall of Fame in 1994.

Born in Oklahoma, Moose's first name actually was Garnett, but no one ever called him that. Like a lot of trainers, Moose liked to play practical jokes on players. We had these two big offensive tackles back in the 1960s named Lane Howell and Bob Brown. Brown was one of the best offensive linemen in Eagles history. He was a five-time All-Pro who was inducted into the Pro Football Hall of Fame in 2004.

One day, Moose called Brown over and told him they were doing a test to determine the durability of offensive linemen late in games. Brown had just gotten out of the shower and was buck naked. Moose asked Brown to blow into the machine on the table. Before he did, Moose told Brown that Howell had scored a 250 on the test. Bob didn't like anybody beating him at anything, so he took about 10 practice breaths, put his hands on the table, and blew as hard as he could into the device. As he did, this plaster-type substance that was hidden under the table blew all over Bob's testicles.

Another Moose story: In 1968 we were supposed to play the first-ever NFL game in Mexico, a preseason game against the Lions. There were a lot of logistics involved for that game. As the Mexican authorities were checking passports with the list of players and personnel we were sending down there, they couldn't find anybody named Moose. Detty signed his name as Moose and everybody called him Moose, but as I mentioned earlier, his actual name was Garnett. The Mexican consulate held up our paperwork. They kept calling Moose "Muss," and they said they couldn't find any "Muss." Finally they figured out his real name was Garnett and we were good to go.

Except that we never ended up making the trip. They cancelled the game at the last minute as we were getting ready to board our flight to Mexico City. This was Thursday, and the game was supposed to be played on Sunday. The Lions ended up flying to Philly and we played the game at Franklin Field after getting the green light from the University of Pennsylvania. It turned out to be hotter in Philly for the game than it was in Mexico, which was one of the reasons we only drew about 12,000 fans for it.

It wasn't a good day. We lost 20–3 and our quarterback, Norm Snead, broke his leg on the first play of the game. But "Muss" was there to help carry him off the field.

Chapter 34
Entering the Hall

There are only 32 teams in the NFL, which means there were only 31 other people who had the job of ticket manger in the NFL at a given time. We were a very close group. We exchanged ideas and had tremendous respect for one another.

In the mid-1990s the Bears' George McCaskey and I came up with the idea of having an annual meeting of the league's ticket directors. It's now a part of the league's annual fall business summit and gives the league's ticket people an opportunity to share ideas.

At the 2007 meeting, which was held in Philly, we were having a discussion on flex scheduling, which the league had gone to a year earlier. Basically, it allowed NBC—which had the rights to our weekly Sunday night game—to switch games in the final seven weeks of the season so it could put a more compelling matchup in prime time.

Anyway, I was sitting there deeply engrossed in the presentation, which was being shown on two giant screens in the room, when the moderator said we were going to take a brief break. When they eventually turned the video back on, the flex-schedule presentation had been replaced by pictures of me. Yes, me. The rest of the league's ticket people surprised me with a tribute. They showed a bunch of pictures of me from over the years, including one of me zip-lining from the top of Lincoln Financial Field. I was surprised, but I loved it. It was great.

The other ticket people gave me a helmet signed by everyone in the room, which I kept in my office until I retired in 2015, and now I keep it in a special place in our home. The whole video was put on the Eagles' website, and many of my friends saw it. I got emails and letters and phone calls from people I went to high school and college with or met in the marines, not to mention former players and coaches.

The tribute was the brainchild of two good friends of mine in the league office, Nancy Behar and Fred Otto. Nancy, who was the NFL's director of broadcast administration, was the woman I used to make name the show tune I was singing back in the day before I'd tell her whether our game was going to be blacked out or not.

Later in 2007 I got another huge thrill when I learned that I had been nominated for the Pro Football Hall of Fame. Yeah, the one in Canton. I joked at the time that Dallas Cowboys owner Jerry Jones, who also was one of the 100 or so nominees that year and eventually was inducted 10 years later, was asking people who the hell this Leo Carlin guy was.

I was all smiles at my induction into the Eagles Hall of Fame.

Former Eagles cornerback and current NFL executive vice president of football operations Troy Vincent and I were inducted together in 2012.

I was nominated for the Hall of Fame eight straight years, until a separate contributor's category was created in 2015. I never was a finalist (final 15), or even a semifinalist (final 25). I probably wasn't even one of the final 50 or even 75. But just being nominated—not once but eight times—was a huge thrill. I mean, I guarantee you it wasn't something I ever predicted when I started working part-time in the Eagles' ticket office back in 1960.

As big a thrill as that 2007 nomination was, it was nothing compared to the one five years later. One day in July 2012, I got a call from Jeffrey Lurie's executive assistant. He told me Jeffrey wanted to talk to me and asked that I be available until 10:00 that night. I usually snooze off a little early, but I can tell you I stayed awake that night. Kay kept asking me, "Is everything all right? Is everything all right?"

I couldn't imagine what Jeffrey wanted. Finally, about quarter to 10:00, the phone rang. It was Jeffrey. I occasionally would get Jeffrey tickets for events. I thought maybe that's why he was calling. So I said to him, "Do you need me to get you tickets for something?" He said, "No, no. That's not why I'm calling, Leo. I just wanted you to hear it from me that we're inducting you into the Eagles Hall of Fame."

Wow. Just wow. I nearly fell out of my chair. I don't know how many times it's physically possible to say "Thank you" in 30 seconds, but I think I broke the record that night. I mean, what do you say when you get the news that you're about to join the likes of Chuck Bednarik, Tom Brookshier, Bill Bergey, Ben Hawkins, Reggie White, Jerome Brown, Harold Carmichael, Ron Jaworski, Tommy McDonald, Wilbert Montgomery, Brian Dawkins, Brian Westbrook, Dick Vermeil, and Steve Van Buren, among others, in the team's Hall of Fame? I was floored,

Several of our 22 grandkids in their Carlin No. 24 jerseys.

On the field with Kay at my 2012 Eagles Hall of Fame induction. What an honor!

absolutely floored. I was moved beyond belief. I loved it. I love him for it. That's pretty cool. I'm eternally grateful to Jeffrey for doing that for me.

The other inductee that year was Troy Vincent, the former Eagles Pro Bowl defensive back who now is the NFL's executive vice president of football operations. Troy and I were honored at halftime of a late-November game at Lincoln Financial Field against Carolina. All of my children and grandchildren were there, as well as countless friends. It was a surreal situation.

I love the Eagles. I love the people that I worked with. I love the fans. I'd see the same names on the season-ticket database year after year after year, though I didn't know whether it was the same people or two or three different generations with the same last name because I had been around so long.

That 2012 season wasn't very memorable for the Eagles. They finished 4–12 and Andy Reid was fired after 14 years. But it will always be special to me.

Chapter 35

The Battle of My Life

Eight years ago, I realized something wasn't quite right. I'd be holding my left arm up, and then it would suddenly go down. I was 73 at the time. I was still active, still working for the Eagles, but I knew something was wrong with me. I went to the doctor and they did a bunch of tests and told me something I didn't want to hear: they said I had Parkinson's.

I had been an active runner and was still running when I first found out about the Parkinson's. I remember saying to myself at the time, "I'm going to beat the shit out of this thing." The first couple of years, it wasn't a big deal. It hadn't reached a point where it was debilitating or I thought it was going to be a problem. It was so negligible early on that, for a while, I thought I *was* beating it. But I'm not.

I never stop hoping they'll find a cure or something that will slow it down. And I never stop fighting this goddamn thing. Now I'm 82. It may beat me, but I'm never, ever going to surrender to it. That's not in my makeup.

I'm a big overdoer. When I played sports, I tended to be pretty aggressive, very competitive. I've been dealing with this disease the same way. I'm still working out five days a week. When I still was with the Eagles, I would work out there. After I retired and before the COVID pandemic, I would go to a Planet Fitness near our house and go to rehab.

I was even taking boxing classes twice a week and doing other exercises. But it's getting tougher and tougher.

It pisses me off that this happened to me. But my approach is, I'm not going to have regrets and think when it's too late that I should've done this or that. I want to do everything I can to deal with it and fight it. I do my level best to get a good night's sleep and wake up refreshed every morning so that I can do my exercises. One thing that has complicated matters is my left foot is in pretty bad shape—not from the Parkinson's but from all of the running I've done in my life. I have arthritis and bone issues with the foot. It makes it hard to go to the gym and work out.

I'm very open about talking about the disease. I'm certainly not ashamed. It happened to me, and I have to deal with it. When I first tell people I have Parkinson's, there's usually this slight delay, kind of like they're embarrassed. But hey, I didn't do anything wrong.

I was talking to my longtime friend John Bunting, who played for both the Eagles and the Stars, a while back and I said, "You know I have Parkinson's, right?" He looked at me and said, "I pity that damn disease. I've played racquetball so many times with you that I know you're going to kick its ass."

The toughest thing about the Parkinson's is the impact it has on me mentally. I'm worried about forgetting things. I was in the Acme not long ago and I saw a woman. She knew me and came running up to talk to me, and I didn't know her name at all. She used to work at my gym, and I apologized to her for forgetting her name.

In 2015, a few years after I was diagnosed with Parkinson's, I decided it was finally time to retire from the Eagles. It was totally my decision. Jeffrey Lurie said I had a place with the organization for as long as I wanted one, which I appreciated very much. But I was 77. I had spent more than a half-century in professional football. I just thought it was best for me and Kay and everybody to call it a career at that point.

I hadn't had any tremors yet from the Parkinson's, and I didn't want to start having them at work. Plus, with everything Kay was going through with her own health, she deserved to have me there with her full-time. Every now and then, she would give me a little nudge and say, "C'mon, Leo. It's my turn." And she was right.

Another reason I decided it was time to retire was I didn't want to be that old guy who hangs around too long. Would it have come to that? Maybe. I was never treated that way. They always treated me well. Jeffrey and I got along wonderfully, but sooner or later, technology probably would've lapped me.

Ironically, I brought technology to the NFL in the 1960s and '70s. But I could see that was becoming more sophisticated too. I wanted to retain my dignity. I wanted to go out on top. I never said that to anybody, I never gave a speech, but it's how I felt.

That doesn't mean I don't miss it. God, I miss it. I miss everything about it. I miss singing to Nancy in the league office. I miss, before computerization took over completely, challenging people to count the tickets faster than me. I miss so much. Working for the Eagles was an absolute blast. It was wonderful, all of it: the characters I've met, the friends I've made over the course of my career, the players and coaches I've had the pleasure of working with, the things I got to experience. It's been a wonderful, wonderful career.

A week after I retired, something really strange happened. We have a deck on the back of our house, off the kitchen. One day, an eagle landed on the deck. It sat there for the longest time before finally flying off. In all the time we'd lived in that house, we had never seen an eagle there. Then I retired and it suddenly appeared. For a week, it kept coming back every day. Is that weird or what?

In my first year with the Eagles in 1960, they won the NFL championship, beating the Green Bay Packers at Franklin Field 17–13 on my first wedding anniversary. The Packers would go on to win five league titles in the 1960s, including the first two Super Bowls, but that day belonged to the Eagles. Chuck Bednarik preserved the win when he

Posing with the Vince Lombardi Trophy following the Eagles' victory in Super Bowl LII. (Inset) I also received a pretty special souvenir from the game.

tackled Packers fullback Jim Taylor at the 10-yard line and then lay on top of Taylor until the clock ran out.

I never imagined then that 57 years would pass before the Eagles would win another championship. They made it to the Super Bowl in 1980 and 2004 but lost both times. I wasn't sure whether I'd still be alive to see them finally win a Super Bowl. Then, in 2017, the drought finally ended. Two years after I retired, in just Doug Pederson's second year as head coach, they shocked the world and beat Bill Belichick and the New England Patriots 41–33 in Super Bowl LII.

The city went completely bonkers. More than 2 million people attended the championship parade down Broad Street. The team invited all of its Hall of Famers to the parade, so I was fortunate enough to have a front-row seat for all of the parade speeches in front of the art museum. It was freezing that day and I ended up getting the flu, which can be dangerous for someone my age. But it was worth it to share in that experience, which had been 57 years in the making.

Not long after that, I got an email from Jeffrey informing me that I was going to be getting a Super Bowl ring. What a thrill that was. After they won the championship, I didn't allow myself to be pompous enough to think I was going to get one. I mean, I no longer worked for the team. But I definitely wanted one, no question about that. When Jeffrey emailed me and told me to go get measured for a ring, I got pretty emotional.

The ring presentation was at the 2300 Arena on Delaware Avenue in South Philly, not far from Lincoln Financial Stadium. It was a first-class event, as you'd expect from anything Jeffrey puts on.

The rings themselves are made of pure 10 karat white gold, adorned with a total of 219 diamonds and 17 rare green sapphires. The Eagles logo is displayed with 52 pavé diamonds, signifying Super Bowl 52. The bezel of the ring features a waterfall of 127 diamonds, which pays tribute to the game's most famous play, the "Philly Special"—tight end Trey Burton's touchdown pass to quarterback Nick Foles. The 127 diamonds represent the sum of the jersey numbers of the three players who handled the football on that fourth-and-1 play at the 1-yard line—Burton, Foles, and running back Corey Clement, who took the direct snap and flipped the ball to Burton, who tossed it to a wide-open Foles. The ring also has four green sapphires that represent the Eagles' four NFL championships in 1948, 1949, 1960, and 2017. And a dog mask—which became the symbol of the 2017 team's underdog mentality—is inscribed on the inside of the ring, along with my signature.

I can't thank Jeffrey Lurie enough for including me in the victory celebration and giving me a Super Bowl ring. He didn't have to do that, but that's the kind of person he is. When they opened the doors to start the ring presentation party, he made a point of finding me and telling me, "Don't forget, Leo. You're a serious part of all of this."

I think about what he said a lot.

What a wonderful ride it has been!